RAF
TRANSPORT COMMAND

A PICTORIAL HISTORY

KEITH WILSON

AMBERLEY

Acknowledgements

A project of this nature requires the help and support of many people, who have contributed in different ways to make the book possible. The author would like to offer his sincere thanks to the following:

To Sebastian Cox at the Air Historical Branch, RAF Northolt for providing the Branch's support with access to the collection of images; along with his encouragement and sense of humour.

To Howard Mason, Barry Guess and Trevor Friend at the BAe Heritage Centre at Farnborough: for allowing me to access to their excellent archive; and their help with images and information.

Special thanks must go to Lee Barton at the Air Historical Branch for his unwavering enthusiasm, vision and attention to detail during the image selection process. Also for his special research skills and tenacity; unearthing new information and responding to the never-ending stream of questions.

At Amberley Publishing, I would like to thank Kevin Paul, Louis Archard and Aaron Phull for their considerable input at key stages during the book's production.

Finally, sincere thanks to my wife Carol and sons Sam and Oliver. Thank you for your patience and support throughout the project. I couldn't have done it without you.

First published 2017

Amberley Publishing
The Hill, Stroud
Gloucestershire, GL5 4EP

www.amberley-books.com

Copyright © Keith Wilson, 2017

The right of Keith Wilson to be identified as the Author of this work has been asserted in accordance with the Copyrights, Designs and Patents Act 1988.

ISBN: 978 1 4456 6598 6 (print)
ISBN: 978 1 4456 6599 3 (ebook)

British Library Cataloguing in Publication Data.
A catalogue record for this book is available from the British Library.

Typeset in 9.5pt on 12pt Celeste.
Typesetting by Amberley Publishing.
Printed in the UK.

Contents

Introduction

Ferio Ferendo – 'I strike by carrying'

When RAF Transport Command was called into existence by Parliamentary proclamation on 25 March 1943, all of its component parts had already been on active service for three and a half years. It was not a new role created for the RAF, as its main activities of transport and ferrying aircraft had already grown significantly under the demands of the Second World War; especially the reinforcement routes that crossed the Atlantic and Africa. UK-based transport squadrons had played a vital and active supporting role in the battles of France and Britain; had carried supplies to beleaguered Malta; while the Middle East Air Force transport wing had operated in close cooperation with the Eighth Army – probably, the first use of integrated air power. Then there were the carriage of the airborne forces for both the Italian and European campaigns of 1943–45.

Air transport had been an integral part of RAF operations in the Middle East since 1920s, because of the vast distances between stations, especially Cairo and Baghdad; and the importance of maintaining communications, especially by the mail service. Air transport took just fourth place in the RAF, behind the demands of bombers, fighters and maritime squadrons during the rearmament programmes of the 1930s.

The only military transport aircraft to enter service with the RAF before the outbreak of the Second World War were dual-purpose bomber-transport aircraft – the Bristol Bombay and Handley Page Harrow – neither of which were utilised as bomber aircraft during the Second World War as they were quickly superseded by more up-to-date designs such as the Hampden, Wellington and Whitley. This lack of suitable transport aircraft was just one reason for the delay in the formation of Transport Command.

When formed in March 1943, the new Command was created from three existing Groups and a Wing: No. 44 Group in the UK; No. 45 (Atlantic Transport) Group (formerly Ferry Command) in Montreal; No. 216 Group in Cairo; and No. 179 (Ferry) Wing in Karachi. The AOC of No. 45 Group, Air Chief Marshal Sir Frederick Bowhill, was appointed Air Officer Commanding-in-Chief.

Air Chief Marshal Sir Frederick Bowhill was appointed Air Officer Commanding-in-Chief of Support Command upon its formation on 25 March 1943. (*Crown Copyright/Air Historical Branch image CH-14503*)

With its component groups in the UK, Canada, Egypt and India, Transport Command had an international status and outlook from the very start. Its official purpose was 'to undertake the responsibility for the organisation and operation of all Service Air Lines, Service Air Movements of freight and personnel, and Overseas and Inter-continental delivery of aircraft by operational ferry air routes'. Interestingly, this official description of its roles said nothing about the military operations in which the new command would soon become involved.

Transport Command went into battle on five occasions during the Second World War. Firstly, they supported the invasion of Sicily in 1943 (Operation Husky), then there was the aborted Dodecanese Islands operation later that year (Operation Accolade), they spearheaded the Allied invasion of Europe in 1944 (Operation Overlord), transported the airborne forces in the ill-fated attempt to capture the bridges at Arnhem in September 1944 (Operation Market), and carried troops across the Rhine in March 1945 for the final push into Nazi Germany (Operation Varsity).

Later, when the war in Europe had been won, Transport Command were involved in a massive trooping operation to reinforce the Far East against the Japanese, before being involved in a significant logistical effort to repatriate British servicemen after the Japanese surrender on 14 August 1945.

At the end of the Second World War, Transport Command was spread far and wide across the globe. However, the thorny question arose of exactly what to do with such a large Command once the hostilities had ceased. Thankfully, there was no question of it being disbanded. An Air Staff paper of 28 May 1945 noted: 'Experience has shown that Air Transport has a lasting place in the RAF which cannot be filled by other forms of transport or by the Merchant Air Fleet.' However, organisational changes had to be made and these will be covered in this book.

One of the major problems suffered after the War was the loss of experienced aircrew and groundcrew, mainly through the demobilisation process. Another problem was the return of aircraft supplied through the Lease-Lend programme – particularly Dakota and Liberator aircraft. The Air Ministry would have to produce new types from British industry to replace them and at the time, only one aircraft – the Handley Page Hastings – was in the pipeline, making its first flight in 1946.

As the title suggests, this is predominately a picture-led volume. In selecting the illustrations for this book I have often been obliged to choose between quality and originality. I have gone to great lengths to include as many 'new' images as possible. Where a poor quality image has been used it is because I decided that the interest value of the subject matter warranted the decision, making it a better choice than a more familiar, previously published image.

Wherever possible, the source of the image has been acknowledged in the caption to each illustration. However, on occasions the widespread practice of copying images may have obscured the true origins of some. This may have led to some image credits in this book being incorrect. If this has occurred, it is completely unintentional and I do apologise.

I have thoroughly enjoyed researching this volume, the first in a new 'Pictorial History' series for Amberley Publishing. I sincerely hope this book – reminiscing about RAF Transport Command in both words and pictures – enlightens, and more importantly, entertains the reader.

Keith Wilson
Ramsey, Cambridgeshire
May 2017

The War Years (1943–45)

A lesser-known but nevertheless essential role of Transport Command was the moving of mail, particularly to the front line. Sergeant H. Stillwell unloads mail bags from the underwing tanks of a Hawker Hurricane IIC of 1697 (Air Despatch Delivery Service) Flight at B2/Bazenville after a mail flight from RAF Northolt. The pilot, Flight Lieutenant W. V. Melbourne, looks on. (*Crown Copyright/Air Historical Branch CL-373*)

On 2 April 1943, the newly formed Command opened its Headquarters at Harrow and on 7 May declared its official title should be Transport Command. Shortly afterwards, on 1 June, its badge and motto 'I strike by carrying' were approved by King George VI and it wasn't long before the new Command began operations.

Its 216 Group squadrons were supporting Operation Husky – the Allied invasion of Sicily – which was mounted on 9/10 July 1943 – and the operation marked the first Allied use of airborne forces in the Second World War. The Transport Command contribution to Operation Husky, through 216 Group, included seven of their squadrons – No. 17 with Ju-52s and No. 28 with Ansons, both of the SAAF; Nos 117 and 267 with Hudsons; No. 173 with Lodestars, No. 216 with Dakotas and No. 230 with Sunderland aircraft.

The ending of the Tunisia campaign and the invasion of Sicily had opened up the Mediterranean reinforcement route for aircraft transiting from the UK to the Middle East and on to India for the build-up of squadrons participating in the Burma campaign.

Transport Command's next role was significantly more active when they participated in Operation Accolade – the Allied invasion of three Dodecanese Islands – Cos, Leros and Samos. However, the operation was a disaster for the Allies despite the very best efforts of twenty-two Dakota aircraft, supported by a few Hudsons. In the end, the operation lost six Dakotas.

Ferrying responsibilities

Meanwhile, Transport Command's ferrying responsibilities were increasing as reinforcements were required in the European, Mediterranean and Far East theatres. By the end of 1943, No. 113 (South Atlantic) Wing had dispatched its 1,000th aircraft – pretty much all of which were American-manufactured types. At the same time, No. 112 (North Atlantic) Wing was busy ferrying machines to the UK for service in the European theatre. This pattern was repeated with 216 Group in the Middle East. With the hard-won successes in the Mediterranean in 1943, the main route for aircraft going into theatre could now operate via Casablanca and the volume of traffic continued to rise.

No. 45 Group had been RAF Ferry Command until it was taken over by Transport Command in April 1943; later being named No. 45 (Transport) Group. It then assumed responsibilities in the North and South Atlantic, and West Indies area. In addition to its considerable ferrying role, the Group was also responsible for VIP transport. All of the wartime conferences of Allied leaders involved airlifts on a significant scale. For example, after the Trident conference in Washington in 1943, Winston Churchill and his immediate party were passengers in the BOAC flying boat *Bristol* while it took five Liberators to transport the other conference delegates across the Atlantic.

One very unusual ferry flight was made between 24 June and 1 July, when a Waco Hadrian I glider, FR579, carrying one and a half tons of freight was towed across to the UK by a Dakota, along with a Catalina for company. The team routed via Goose Bay, Bluie West 1 and Reykjavik to Prestwick.

By August 1943, Canadian-built Mosquito aircraft started to come across the Atlantic and it was inevitable that some record crossing times would be set. On 10 May 1944, two Mosquito aircraft crossed to Ballykelly in just 6 hours and 46 minutes, runway-to-runway, or 5 hours and 39½ minutes coast-to-coast. In October 1944, this time was beaten by one minute and by May 1945 the crossing time had been further reduced to 5½ hours. Then, on 23 October 1944, assisted by a 70 mph tail wind, a PR Mosquito of 540 Squadron flew from Gander to St Mawgan in just 5 hours and 10 minutes.

Preparation for the Allied Landings

During the beginning of 1944, 46 Group – the European Transport Support Group – was formed at a time when the Allied landings in Europe were being planned. The new Group was allocated three airfields in the Cotswolds – Blakehill Farm, Broadwell and Down Ampney. It was intended to have five squadrons but in the event only three were formed – 271, 512 and 575 Squadrons. All were to be equipped with Dakota aircraft, with 150 aircraft earmarked for the Group. The choice of airfields had been determined by the close proximity to each other in order to spearhead the Allied airborne assault as part of Operation Overlord, and to be within range of north-west France for a Dakota with Horsa glider in tow. Unfortunately, all three airfields were unfinished, although the runways were complete and certain services had been installed. Consequently, the new 46 Group had a difficult beginning with D-Day and the first landings in Normandy only four months away.

The other newly formed Group in Transport Command was No. 47 – nicknamed 'the trunk route Group' – which began operations on 1 January 1945. With its headquarters at RAF Hendon, the Group assumed the responsibilities of No. 116 Wing, namely the organisation and control of long-range and VIP transport in the RAF. At the end of February 1945, 47 Group had five squadrons and a flight – Nos 24 (the VIP squadron), 246, 511, 525, the Metropolitan Communications Squadron and No. 1680 (T) Flight. The VIP transport role for which 47 Group held responsibility can be illustrated by two journeys in early 1945. On 19 February Douglas Skymaster EW990 arrived at Lyneham, having flown from Cairo non-stop in 13 hours 42 minutes carrying the Prime Minister home from the Three Power Conference at Yalta. Then, on 23 March, the Prime Minister and the Chief of the Imperial General Staff flew from Northolt to Venlo, the Netherlands, in a Dakota of 24 Squadron. The visit coincided with the opening of the 21st Army Group offensive and the crossing of the Rhine on the northern sector of the Western front. The Prime Minister and the CIGS returned to Northolt on 26 March.

Flt Lt David Lord VC

There is insufficient space in this volume to describe fully the considerable contribution made by 46 Group of Transport Command to the major European airborne operations of 1944–45 in Operations Overlord, Market Garden and Varsity. However, the individual act of great heroism on 19 September 1944 over Arnhem in Operation Market (the air aspect of Market Garden) earned Transport Command's only Victoria Cross, awarded posthumously to Flt Lt David Lord of 271 Squadron.

Part of the citation for his Victoria Cross is detailed below:

He was pilot and captain of a Dakota aircraft detailed to drop supplies at Arnhem on the afternoon of 19 September 1944. Our airborne troops had been surrounded and were being pressed into a small area defended by a large number of anti-aircraft guns. Aircrews were warned that intense opposition would be met over the dropping zone. To ensure accuracy they were ordered to fly at 900-feet when dropping their containers.

While flying at 1,500-feet near Arnhem the starboard wing of Flight Lieutenant Lord's aircraft was twice hit by anti-aircraft fire. The starboard engine was set on fire. He would have been justified in leaving the main stream of supply aircraft and continuing at the same height or even abandoning his aircraft. But on learning that his crew were uninjured and that the dropping zone would be reached in three minutes he said he would complete his mission, as the troops were in dire need of supplies.

By now the starboard engine was burning furiously. Flt Lt Lord came down to 900-feet where he was singled out for the concentrated fire of all the anti-aircraft guns. On reaching the dropping zone he kept the aircraft on a straight and level course while supplies were dropped. At the end of the run, he was told that two containers remained.

Although he must have known that the collapse of the starboard wing could not be long delayed, Flt Lt Lord circled, rejoined the main stream of aircraft and made a second run to drop the remaining supplies. These manoeuvres took eight minutes in all, the aircraft being continuously under heavy anti-aircraft fire.

His task completed, Flt Lt Lord ordered his crew to abandon the Dakota, making no attempt himself to leave the aircraft, which was down to 500-feet. A few seconds later, the starboard wing collapsed and the aircraft fell in flames. There was only one survivor, who was flung out while assisting other members of the crew to put on their parachutes.

By continuing his mission in a damaged and burning aircraft, descending to drop the supplies accurately, returning to the dropping zone a second time and, finally, remaining at the controls to give his crew a chance to escape, Flt Lt Lord displayed supreme valour and self-sacrifice. There could be no finer example of sustained courage and determination by a transport pilot on air supply operations.

In summing up the wartime achievements of Transport Command over less than two and a half years, the official history records that its transport aircraft – taking no account of reinforcement and ferry flights – 'flew more than one million hours between 1 April 1943 and the end of the war'.

Three Lockheed Hudson VI transport aircraft (FK507/KW-S, EW889/KW-E and EW887/KW-C), of 267 Squadron based at LG224/Cairo West, Egypt, flying troops to Castel Benito, Tripoli, on an Operation Helpful flight on 9 April 1943. (*Crown Copyright/Air Historical Branch CM-5016*)

A Waco Hadrian I glider, FR579 *Voodoo*, on the ground at Dorval, near Montreal, Canada, before being towed across the Atlantic by a Douglas Dakota of Transport Command in June 1943. The hinged nose of the glider is open for loading the freight to be carried, including 3,360 lbs of medical supplies and engine and radio parts. The flight was accomplished in four legs. On 23 June 1943 the Dakota/Hadrian combination flew from Duval to Goose Bay, Labrador. Four days later, the pair headed for Greenland and after another three-day break, the glider was towed across to Iceland after a flight of 7 hours. On 1 July, they flew the final leg, landing at Prestwick. (*Crown Copyright/Air Historical Branch CH-10465*)

British Army casualties on stretchers wait to be loaded into Lockheed Lodestar 1371, an ambulance aircraft of the South African Air Force, at Catania, Sicily, for evacuation to hospitals in North Africa, during Operation Husky in July 1943. (*Crown Copyright/Air Historical Branch CNA-1110*)

Consolidated Liberator I, AL578 *Marco Polo*, of 45 (Atlantic Transport) Group, being loaded for a transatlantic flight on the Return Ferry Service at Dorval, near Montreal, Canada, in November 1943. (*Crown Copyright/Air Historical Branch CH-14619*)

A Martin Baltimore IV taxies to its dispersal in a cloud of dust after landing at Accra on the Gold Coast, while flying the South Atlantic ferry route from Nassau, Bahamas, to Cairo in December 1943. This aircraft had the long-range fuel tank fitted under the fuselage. (*Crown Copyright/Air Historical Branch CH-14632*)

Albemarle ST.I Series 2, P1514, of 511 Squadron based at RAF Lyneham on 7 September 1943. This was one of six Mark I aircraft modified to 'Lyneham Standard' transport configuration for use on the Lyneham–Gibraltar–Algiers route by 'C' Flight of the Squadron. (*Crown Copyright/ Air Historical Branch CH-12049*)

American-built aircraft lined up at Dorval airport near Montreal, Canada, while awaiting delivery to the United Kingdom via the North Atlantic air route in December 1943. During the war, Dorval airport became the major transit point in North America for flights to Europe and was the Headquarters of 45 (Atlantic Transport) Group (formerly the Atlantic Ferry Organisation). (*Crown Copyright/Air Historical Branch CH-13918*)

Aircraft parked at the Transport Command Staging Post at Lagens in December 1943. In the foreground is the tail of a Douglas C-54A Skymaster of USAAF Air Transport Command, and in the background a Consolidated Liberator B.VI of the RAF, being ferried from the United States to the United Kingdom for operational service. (*Crown Copyright/Air Historical Branch CA-139*)

Grumman Goose I, MV993, of 24 Squadron based at RAF Hendon, photographed in flight during 1942. This aircraft was formerly G-AFKJ and was owned by Lord Beaverbrook before being impressed into RAF service. It was taken on charge at Speke and then issued to HQ ATA on 21 August 1942 before transferring to 24 Squadron on 2 February 1943. Later, it joined the Metropolitan Communication Squadron at RAF Hendon on 26 January 1945 but, sadly, was written off while landing at Calshot on 2 September 1945 when the aircraft capsized after a wingtip float broke off. (*Crown Copyright/Air Historical Branch CH-6901*)

A mixed service and civilian crew of No. 45 Group, RAF leaves their Consolidated Liberator B Mark VI on arriving at Celone, Italy, after a ferry flight from Canada in April 1944. The aircraft were flown directly to the Italian theatre to equip the newly formed No. 31 Squadron SAAF. (*Crown Copyright/Air Historical Branch CNA-2784*)

The crew of a BOAC Consolidated Liberator is briefed by an officer of Transatlantic Flying Control in the Operations Room at Prestwick, in April 1944. (*Crown Copyright/ Air Historical Branch CH-14368*)

Tipper trucks removing earth from the site of the new main runway at Heathrow, on 19 April 1944. Although originally developed as an airfield for RAF Transport Command on the site of the Great West Road (or Harmondsworth) aerodrome, Heathrow was later selected as the location of London's new post-war airport. (*Crown Copyright/Air Historical Branch CH-18206*)

Douglas Dakota aircraft of 233 Squadron, part of No. 46 Group, lined up on the perimeter track at Blakehill Farm, Wiltshire, ahead of an exercise with the 6th Airborne Division on 20 April 1944. (*Crown Copyright/Air Historical Branch CH-12833*)

Vickers Warwick C.1, BV255/O, of 525 Squadron based at RAF Lyneham, photographed on 22 April 1944. This aircraft was originally one of fourteen Warwick transport aircraft converted for use by BOAC (with whom it was registered as G-AGFJ), but which reverted back to RAF service in September 1943. Following service with 525 Squadron, the aircraft later served with 167 and 304 (Polish) Squadrons. (*Crown Copyright/Air Historical Branch CH-12920*)

Aerial photograph of Prestwick Airport, seen from 26,500 feet in April 1944. This image shows the airport at the peak of its wartime development. Ferry traffic can be seen located all around the airport. (*Crown Copyright/Air Historical Branch C-5453*)

Consolidated LB-30 Liberator AL504 *Commando*, the personal transport of the Prime Minister, photographed at RAF Northolt on 8 May 1944 after returning to the United Kingdom, following extensive modification and a complete overhaul by the Consolidated Aircraft Company at San Diego, California. The main changes to the original airframe involved the fitting of a large single rudder and fin, and the extension of the fuselage by 7 feet. The interior was furnished to accommodate twenty passengers and was fitted with bunks and a steward's galley. AL504 flew with the Communications Squadron of No. 45 (Atlantic Transport) Group, Transport Command, until disappearing over the South Atlantic while flying from the Azores to Ottawa, Canada, on 26 May 1945. (*Crown Copyright/Air Historical Branch CH-18793*)

Aircraft assembled at RAF Tarrant Rushton on the afternoon of 6 June 1944 while being prepared for the reinforcement of the British airborne assault during Operation Mallard. On the runway are General Aircraft Hamilcar heavy-lift gliders, preceded by two Airspeed Horsa troop-carrying gliders. Parked on each side of them are Handley Page Halifax glider tugs of 298 and 644 Squadrons. (*Crown Copyright/Air Historical Branch CL-26*)

A member of the ground crew checks the fixings of the freight pannier fitted into the belly of a Warwick C.III of 525 Squadron before it departs Lyneham for a sortie on 4 August 1944. The squadron only operated the Warwick for a very brief period – during the summer of 1944 – mainly on freight tasks. (*Crown Copyright/Air Historical Branch CH-18216*)

No. 267 Squadron made remarkable contributions to the air war in both the Mediterranean and the Burma campaign. Here, Douglas Dakota III aircraft of No. 267 Squadron were photographed while unloading supplies for the Allied forces at Araxos, Greece, in October 1944. The activity drew considerable attention from the local population. (*Crown Copyright/Air Historical Branch CM-5915*)

A USAAF ferry crew hand over a Martin Baltimore V to Flight Lieutenant A. N. Buell of Number 45 (Atlantic Transport) Group at Windsor Field, Nassau, Bahamas, in early 1945. From Nassau, the Baltimore would have been flown to the Mediterranean theatre of operations, via the South Atlantic ferry route. The aircraft was fitted with a long-range fuel tank under the fuselage. (*Crown Copyright/Air Historical Branch CH-14624*)

Aerial view of the Transport Command Delivery Park on the Northeast Apron at Prestwick airport on 25 February 1945, showing aircraft being marshalled after having being flown across the Atlantic. Among the aircraft are Consolidated Liberators, Douglas Dakotas, North American Mitchells, and Canadian-built Avro Lancaster B.Xs. (*Crown Copyright/Air Historical Branch CH-17840*)

Douglas Dakota III aircraft of 267 Squadron lined up at Bari, Italy, in early 1945. Aircraft nearest the camera are (front to rear): KG496/AI, FL589 and FD957. (*Crown Copyright/Air Historical Branch CNA-3333*)

The prototype civilian Avro Lancastrian, VB873, photographed in flight during early 1945. This aircraft was re-registered as G-AGLF and used by BOAC on the London–Sydney 'Kangaroo Route' – a joint venture with Transport Command – which began on 31 May 1945. (*Crown Copyright/Air Historical BranchPRB-1-797*)

Above left: Handley Page Halifax and Short Stirling aircraft tow Airspeed Horsa gliders over the French countryside shortly after crossing the English Channel, en route to the landing zones east of the River Rhine during Operation Varsity on 24 March 1945. (*Crown Copyright/Air Historical Branch CL-2231*)

Above right: Douglas Dakota IV, KN427/AY, of 437 Squadron leads a formation of Dakota aircraft over Copenhagen, while taking a SHAEF Mission to Denmark on 7 May 1945. (*Crown Copyright/ Air Historical Branch CL-2598*)

Another image from Operation Varsity. Douglas Dakota aircraft of 46 Group fly in formation over Wavre, Belgium, heading for the dropping zones east of the River Rhine on 24 March 1945. Above them, more Dakota aircraft towing Airspeed Horsa gliders fly a divergent course towards their objectives. (*Crown Copyright/Air Historical Branch CL-2242*)

Consolidated Coronado I JX501 *Beaumaris* of 231 Squadron based at Dorval, Canada, undergoing a major inspection at the Marine Base, Bermuda, in mid-1945. The aircraft was one of ten delivered to the squadron for use on long-distance passenger and freight operations. It was scuttled off Largs, Ayrshire, on 28 March 1946. (*Crown Copyright/Air Historical Branch CH-15944*)

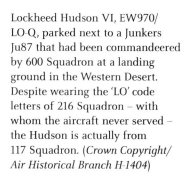

The Prime Minister, Winston Churchill, accompanied by Air Marshal the Hon. Sir Ralph Cochrane, Air Officer Commanding in Chief Transport Command, walks from his Douglas Skymaster I, EW999, at RAF Northolt upon his return from the Three Power Conference at Potsdam in July 1945. (*Crown Copyright/Air Historical Branch CL-3159*)

Lockheed Hudson VI, EW970/ LO-Q, parked next to a Junkers Ju87 that had been commandeered by 600 Squadron at a landing ground in the Western Desert. Despite wearing the 'LO' code letters of 216 Squadron – with whom the aircraft never served – the Hudson is actually from 117 Squadron. (*Crown Copyright/ Air Historical Branch H-1404*)

Returning the Troops

Two ambulance-fitted Dominie aircraft of 24 Squadron. Both were former de Havilland DH.89A Dragon Rapide aircraft impressed into RAF service. In the foreground is Z7258, presented to the RAF by the Silver Thimble Fund and named *Women of the Empire* by Lady Maud Carnegie. On the left is Z7261, similarly named *Women of Britain*. (*Crown Copyright/Air Historical Branch CH-2729*)

Before the end of 1944 the Chiefs of Staff had approved a policy of large-scale air trooping after the anticipated defeat of Germany. This programme was initiated to support Operation Dracula (originally referred to as Vanguard), a seaborne and airborne attack on Rangoon proposed by Admiral Lord Louis Mountbatten, Commander-in-Chief, South-East Asia. The Air Ministry and War Office had mistakenly assumed a planning date of 30 June 1945 for the defeat of Germany, and anticipated that the UK–India air trooping would begin in July with an initial transfer of 3,500 troops, increasing to 17,500 by October. The purpose of this trooping was to accelerate the redeployment for the war against Japan, whether or not Dracula was postponed or was carried out in a modified form. Clearly, the repatriation programme was not going to be a one-way business.

The act of military surrender was signed in Reims on 7 May 1945 and on the following day in Berlin. A public holiday was celebrated on 8 May 1945, simply known as VE Day (Victory in Europe Day), and in London crowds flocked to Trafalgar Square, Piccadilly Circus and Whitehall to celebrate the unconditional surrender of Germany. The event was similarly celebrated in France, the Czech Republic, Slovakia, Latvia, Lithuania and Estonia.

Repatriation programme

A massive repatriation programme was organised with Transport Command at the forefront of operations. It wasn't just a simple case of returning the Allied troops back home now that the fighting had ceased. There were all of the Allied prisoners of war, along with millions of people who had merely been displaced as a result of Second World War; not least of which were people who had been placed in camps far away from their own countries purely based upon their religious beliefs. Thousands of children affected by the concentration camps were brought to Britain for rehabilitation. This massive repatriation effort continued for the next four months. Transport Command was assisted by aircraft and crews from Bomber Command (including Halifax and Stirling aircraft) in carrying out the massive airlift.

However, immediately after VJ Day on 2 September 1945, an Air Ambulance Trooping Programme was initiated. So great was the importance placed on returning all Allied officers and men that almost half of Bomber Command's aircraft were temporarily transferred to Transport Command to assist with the task.

On 16 September 1945, the Chief of the Air Staff (Sir Charles Portal) wrote to the Commander-in-Chief Transport Command, the Rt Hon Sir Ralph Cochrane, to say that 'the air trooping programme will make a real contribution to the economic revival of the country'.

The repatriation effort was a slick operation. Facilities en route, while not of a five-star standard, were extremely efficiently organised and when an aircraft landed, it would be refuelled, any unserviceability would be checked and rectified, the aircraft's position and load would be signalled to the next destination, and the crew and passengers fed as normally a slip crew was ready to take the aircraft on after two hours on the ground. Meanwhile, the incoming crew would be transferred to their transit accommodation. Any aircraft which suffered a major defect and required spare parts became a so-called 'Aircraft on Ground' (AOG) and an urgent message would be sent for those spare parts to be delivered as soon as was possible. This procedure applied to all Transport Command aircraft en route – Liberators, Yorks, Halifaxes, Stirlings and Dakotas – in the Large Scale Trooping Operation.

To provide some idea of the scale of the operations involved at the main staging post at RAF Mauripur (located four miles north-west of Karachi), the number of movements involved during November 1945 was 361 aircraft arrived from the west, while 375 flights departed from there en route to the UK.

Airmen go on strike

During January 1946, two related events occurred, in the UK and in India. Firstly, the Government decided to reduce large scale air trooping; and then airmen of 229 Group went on strike – a reaction by those on the ground who felt their role of assisting repatriation of other Army and RAF personnel meant that their own repatriation was being delayed so that they could support and effect the airlift. More importantly, they feared that by the time they themselves were returned to the UK, all of the civilian jobs would have been taken by those that they had helped to send on ahead.

The AOC of 229 Group, Air Commodore G. T. Jarman DSO DFC, was sent to Mauripur, where he arrived to inspect the base on 20 January 1946. During the following few days, Jarman held meetings with the striking airmen. Their grievances within the unit were varied but in general they centred on repatriation and demobilisation.

On the evening of 23 January, Air Marshal Carr addressed a large meeting of British Other Ranks and he assured them that their demands had reached the highest quarters. It seemed likely that the men would agree to return to work, had not someone announced that other 229 Group units and stations under 216 Group were on strike. A further meeting was held with the men on 24 January and eventually they returned to work on 25 January, although during the period of the unrest, both Trooping and Traffic Routes and Internal Airline Squadrons were all kept going by officers and senior NCOs.

During January–March 1946, the trooping operations gradually diminished.

In a public tribute to the air transport role of his Command during the war years, Sir Ralph Cochrane said that in the twenty-one-month period from the beginning of 1945 to the end of September 1946, the RAF had flown more passenger miles that than had British civil aviation in all of its twenty-one years' existence.

Leading Aircraftwoman Pearl Bradburn, a WAAF nursing orderly from Sale, Cheshire, writing out medical transport tags for her patients, wounded soldiers on board a Douglas Dakota at B2/ Bazenville, Normandy, before they are flown back to the UK. (*Crown Copyright/Air Historical Branch CL-416*)

Indian troops waiting to board Vickers Wellington X, HZ950/Z, of 99 Squadron, on an airfield in India in May 1944. A detachment of the squadron undertook emergency supply-dropping and bomb-transportation duties with Troop Carrier Command during the siege of Imphal. (*Crown Copyright/Air Historical Branch CF-154*)

A Handley Page Harrow II transport ambulance aircraft, K6984/BJ-E, of the 271 Squadron Detachment at RAF Hendon. Frequently known as the 'Sparrow', two of 271 Squadron's Harrows helped to evacuated wounded troops from Arnhem in September 1944. (*Crown Copyright/ Air Historical Branch CH-11520*)

Medical orderlies loading stretcher cases into Harrow II ambulance aircraft K6984/BJ-E of the 271 Squadron Detachment at RAF Hendon. (*Crown Copyright/Air Historical Branch CH-11522*)

The interior of Harrow II K6984/BJ-E of 271 Squadron, showing the special modifications installed for the carrying of a large number of stretcher cases. (*Crown Copyright/Air Historical Branch CH-11523*)

Above and below: Liberated Allied prisoners of war wait at an airfield in Belgium before boarding a line of Short Stirling aircraft (those in the foreground belonging to 299 Squadron) for repatriation to the UK in April 1945. (*Crown Copyright/Air Historical Branch CL-2428, CL-2433*)

RAF Stirling aircraft were used to relieve some of the suffering of the war. As well as returning Czechoslovaks to their own country, the Stirling aircraft also returned to Britain with hundreds of Czechoslovak children; orphans who had been in concentration camps during the German occupation and who were being brought to Britain for rehabilitation. In this image, some of the children walk towards a line of 196 Squadron Stirling IV aircraft, including LK242/ZO-A, which had arrived in Prague earlier in the day to take them to the reception centre at Crosby-on-Eden, near Carlisle, on 13 August 1945. (*Crown Copyright/Air Historical Branch CH-15899*)

A small group of Czechoslovak children, orphans from the concentration camps, being unloaded in the UK after their flight in a Stirling IV of 196 Squadron from Prague. (*Crown Copyright/Air Historical Branch CH-15903*)

Liberated Allied prisoners-of-war from camps in Thailand, waiting to board Douglas Dakotas of RAF Transport Command at Don Muang airfield, Bangkok, for their flight to Rangoon, Burma, in September 1945. (*Crown Copyright/Air Historical Branch CF-733*)

Released Allied prisoners of war alighting from an RAF Transport Command Dakota aircraft at Mingaladon airfield, Rangoon, after their flight from Den Muang airfield near Bangkok in early September 1945. (*Crown Copyright/Air Historical Branch CI-1600*)

Jimmy Cairns, a five-and-a-half-year-old civilian internee, is seen sitting on his luggage after just having been flown to Singapore by RAF Transport Command. Jimmy, whose mother was killed when the boat in which they were trying to leave Malaya was sunk, spent eight hours in the water before being picked up. Jimmy and his father spent the war in a camp for civilian internees in Sumatra. (*Crown Copyright/Air Historical Branch CI-1676*)

Civilian internees leave an RAF Transport Command Dakota aircraft in which they were flown from Sumatra to Singapore. (*Crown Copyright/Air Historical Branch CI-1677*)

Medical orderlies of the Casualty Air Evacuation Unit carry a sick Dutch internee from an RAF Transport Command Dakota aircraft at Batavia in Java in November 1945. (*Crown Copyright/ Air Historical Branch CF-880*)

A casualty from the fighting in Normandy is loaded from an Army ambulance into one of the Dakota IIIs of 46 Group at B2/Bazenville, Normandy, for evacuation to the UK. (*Crown Copyright/Air Historical Branch CL-3884*)

Another view of Dakota IIIs of 46 Group at B2/Bazenville, Normandy, loading casualties for evacuation to the UK. Identifiable aircraft include KG432/H of 512 Squadron (centre), and KG320/B1 of 575 Squadron (extreme right). (*Crown Copyright/ Air Historical Branch CL-3885*)

Aircraft of Transport Command parked at Prague airport, during preparations for the welcome of returning Czechoslovakian Air Force squadrons which formerly served with the RAF. Parked in the foreground are Douglas Dakotas of 46 and 47 Groups, which operated a regular air service from Croydon to Prague. Standing out from its contemporaries on the ramp is VVIP Dakota IV KN386, often used by the Royal Family and one of a number of the type operated by 24 Squadron. Behind them are Short Stirling aircraft of 38 Group, which were being used to repatriate Czechoslovaks from the United Kingdom back to their homeland. (*Crown Copyright/Air Historical Branch CL-3330*)

Although Britain had ended the Second World War as one of the victorious Allies, the country was almost bankrupt after the vast outlay of national resources during the War. The first years of peace were blighted by rationing and austerity which exceeded those of the war years. Severe financial problems coupled with the debilitating effect of nearly six years of war made the task of redirecting the nation's war-making capacity to meet civilian peacetime needs very difficult.

In September 1945, Transport Command was a huge organisation consisting of ten Groups, twenty-four Wings, seven airports, 103 stations world-wide and fifty-five squadrons. Some of these squadrons had been in the transport role pre-war or since the early days of hostilities, Nos 24, 216 and 271 for example; some were former Bomber or Coastal Command squadrons (238 and 242 Squadrons); some even had former Fighter Command squadron numbers. However, the very large majority of the squadrons had been formed during the war years. In addition to its 103 stations, Transport Command also had 163 staging posts, along with many other units located at 336 places throughout the world – it was a truly global operation.

Transport Command's contribution to the war effort had been varied: the transport of passengers and freight, ferrying reinforcement aircraft to battle areas, airborne forces operations with the Army, and trooping to the Far East theatre. In addition, there was the rarely seen but morale-boosting carriage of mail to the troops in Europe, utilising specially modified Hurricane and Spitfire aircraft.

Inevitably, some of these roles ceased with the ending of hostilities, like the ferrying of Lease-Lend. However, there was still a significant requirement for the air-movement of Service passengers and for aircraft to be sent to the Middle East and India. Furthermore, the Army still required RAF support for parachute training.

Transport Command had made itself so useful it could not be ignored; but its responsibilities clearly needed to be redefined and its activities would reduce dramatically in size from the wartime dimensions. There was no question of Transport Command being disbanded. In fact, their role was recognised in an Air Staff paper of 28 May 1945, which said: 'Experience has shown that Air Transport has a lasting place in the RAF which cannot be filled by other forms of transport or by the Merchant Air Fleet.' At the time, Transport Command was busy with repatriating DPs (displaced persons) within Europe, and was also involved with the trooping task ahead of the Japanese surrender in August 1945.

Post-war downsizing

Once hostilities had come to an end, the Air Council met to consider the Transport Command organisation. While its wartime activities were recognised, it was recommended that Transport Command be brought into line with normal RAF practice and that responsibilities be re-allocated. It meant a significant downsizing of the Command.

By 19 February 1946, the subsequent changes had resulted in the Command being reduced to an establishment of 47½ squadrons and flights, with 40½ of them being operational. However, the organisers had already warned of further reorganisations and reductions by 1 March 1946. Included were plans to transfer the control of Transport formations and services in overseas theatres (including the British Air Force of Occupation in Germany) from Transport Command to Overseas Theatre Commanders, retaining in Transport Command the home-based formations and units, along with the control of all 'trunk' services.

By 15 March, the Order of Battle showed a total establishment of just 24½ established squadrons, of which 19½ were operational. Instead of a total unit establishment of 1,174 aircraft worldwide, Transport Command now retained just 541 aircraft. Savage cuts indeed! Transport Command had relied heavily on US-built aircraft, particularly Liberator and Dakota aircraft. In the mid-March 1946 Order of Battle, the total strength for these two types was 125 and 232 respectively. With the end of Lease-Lend looming, these would all have to be replaced by British aircraft. Thankfully, the Dakota aircraft continued in service for many more years, and eight squadrons were heavily utilised during the Berlin Airlift.

Avro York aircraft had made a slow entry into Transport Command service, the first special VIP-equipped aircraft having joined in March 1943. However, with production concentrated on the Lancaster bomber, the first 'standard' York C.1, MW104, was delivered to 511 Squadron at RAF Lyneham on 10 February 1944. Eventually, eight squadrons (Nos 24, 40, 51, 59, 99, 206, 242 and 511 squadrons) were equipped with the York C.1 and all of them participated in the Berlin Airlift.

Elsewhere, Liberator squadrons were being disbanded as the aircraft had to be returned to the USA following the conclusion of the Lease-Lend arrangement and most had returned by the middle of 1946. However, a shortage of aircraft was not the only problem suffered by Transport

Command. The demobilisation process was leaving the Command seriously short in many specialised branches, including air crews, aircraft maintenance and even medical staff.

Dakota replacement required

The next big problem was the Douglas Dakota aircraft supplied to the RAF under the Lease-Lend scheme. Having served both in the air support role and also on the trunk routes for trooping, these too were due to be returned. The Air Council discussed the matter at a meeting on 8 September 1947 when the importance of proceeding with the Vickers Valetta production was realised as this type would eventually replace the Dakota. It was realised by the meeting that the Dakota aircraft were still costing dollars which the country clearly could not afford. There were even discussions on accelerating the Valetta production but in the end this option was not proceeded with.

The prototype Valetta (VL249) would eventually make its first flight on 30 June 1947, with the first production Valetta C.1 aircraft (VL262) flying on 28 January 1948. The first aircraft entered service with number 204 Squadron at Kabrit in Egypt in May 1949 and they eventually supplanted the Dakota in Transport Command service, as well as both the Middle and Far East Forces.

In the meantime, sufficient Dakota aircraft were retained to equip eight squadrons in Transport Command and it was just as well that they did! During a period of long-term strategic planning and financial stringency, a major crisis blew up, which was to test the resolve and transport capabilities of both the RAF and the USAF – the Berlin Airlift.

Looking slightly worse for wear, Anson C.XII PH693 of 167 Squadron based at RAF Blackbushe, was photographed while visiting RAF Hendon during late September 1945. The last two letters ('GF') of its four-letter Transport Command call-sign 'OAGF' can be seen painted on the nose of the aircraft. (*Crown Copyright/Air Historical Branch CH-16493*)

The interior of Avro Anson C.XII PH693 of 167 Squadron; looking forward from the passenger compartment to the cockpit. The aircraft's four-letter Transport Command call-sign 'OAGF' can be seen painted on the instrument panel to the right. (*Crown Copyright/Air Historical Branch CH-16482*)

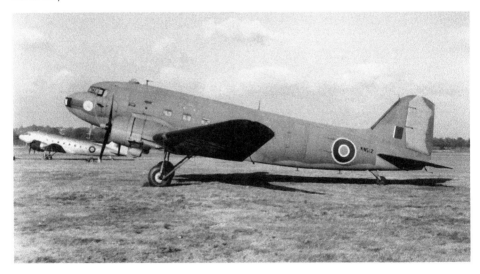

Dakota IV KN512 of 24 Squadron parked at RAF Hendon in late September 1945. The aircraft is camouflaged but bears post-war Transport Command markings with the serial number being painted on the undersides of the wings, and the Transport Command badge and aircraft call-sign displayed on the nose. (*Crown Copyright/Air Historical Branch CH-16494*)

Liberator C.I AL578 *Marco Polo* of 45 (Atlantic Transport) Group, on the ground at RAF Lyneham in September 1945. This long-serving aircraft is seen in Transport Command's post-war finish, consisting of overall polished bare-metal surfaces, with the serial number painted under each wing and the aircraft call-sign displayed on the nose. Taken on charge on 12 January 1943, AL578 served with Transport Command until 7 January 1946 when it was transferred to BOAC and cannibalised for spares. (*Crown Copyright/Air Historical Branch CH-16497*)

The interior of the passengers' compartment of a Consolidated Liberator C.I, looking forward. (*Crown Copyright/Air Historical Branch CH-16486*)

Lancastrian C.2 VM734, photographed while serving with the Transport Command Aircrew Examining Centre at RAF Bramcote in July 1946. (*Crown Copyright/Air Historical Branch R-93*)

As part of a plan to create the Airborne Medical Services, a course was run by the Transport Command Development Unit at the Number 1 Parachute and Glider Training School (part of 38 Group) at RAF Upper Heyford in September 1948. The concept was to train medically qualified staff to be capable of parachuting into incidents requiring their immediate care.

In this image, a group are packing a special medical support pack, dropped with the parachutists, to provide the delicate medical equipment required to support the medical team. (*Crown Copyright/ Air Historical Branch R-1925a*)

The first four parachute-borne nurses were all members of the Princess Mary's RAF Nursing Service and their course included all aspects of the normal parachute training, including jumps from both static balloons and Dakota IV aircraft. All four nurses used the 28-foot diameter British Statichute parachute and wore rubber jumping hats. Sister M. M. Bradley from County Tyrone was one of the first four nursing sisters to qualify. (*Crown Copyright/Air Historical Branch R-1920*)

Hastings C.1 TG530 of 47 Squadron, RAF Dishforth, shortly after the squadron re-equipped with the type in November 1948. TG530 was photographed landing back at RAF Fairford following an air test. (*Crown Copyright/Air Historical Branch R-1957*)

The Transport Command Major Servicing Unit were based at RAF Honington as part of 47 Group. In this image, taken in January 1949, a Rolls-Royce Merlin engine is seen being worked on by one of the unit's technicians. (*Crown Copyright/Air Historical Branch R-2079*)

Another view of activities with the Transport Command Major Servicing Unit at RAF Honington in January 1949. Here, a Rolls-Royce Merlin engine is being loaded into Dakota IV KN274 in what is probably a training scenario, as the four wheels located to the left of the image appear to be training aids. (*Crown Copyright/Air Historical Branch R-2105*)

Operation Plainfare – The Berlin Airlift

Air traffic control at Wunstorf had to cope with a larger flow of traffic than ever before. Here, Aircraftsman Charles Currie, an air traffic control assistant, flashes a green Aldis lamp to the first of a wave of Dakota aircraft to signal that they may now taxi from the apron to the runway for a massed departure on 16 September 1948. (*Crown Copyright/Air Historical Branch R-1774*)

At the end of the Second World War, the Allies partitioned the defeated Germany into a Soviet-occupied zone, an American-occupied zone, a British-occupied zone and a French-occupied zone. Berlin, the German capital city, was located deep in the Soviet-occupied zone, and it too was divided into four sections.

Headquarters of the British Air Forces of Occupation (BAFO) was first concerned with the air supply of Berlin on 4 April 1948. It was then that the Headquarters British Army of the Rhine asked what their reactions would be to a proposal that the British Forces in Berlin should be supplied by air, in the event of a blockade of the city. They estimated the requirement to be a lift of 68 tons daily, based on feeding around 10,000.

The Air Ministry were informed and asked if planning could proceed. It was expected the operation would be required to continue for at least one month. On 10 April Air Ministry approval was received and a conference held at HQ BAFO on 15 April to discuss the project.

Operation Knicker

At that meeting held at the Headquarters of the BAFO in Germany on 15 April 1948, the preparation of plans for the air supply of the British Zone in Berlin was discussed. The estimated requirement was a daily airlift of 174,080 lb of food, fuel, ordnance and medical supplies. If an emergency situation arose, this daily estimate would increase by a further 130,050 lb. It was anticipated that two squadrons of Dakota aircraft (twenty-eight in total) would be required to carry out thirty-five to forty sorties a day to complete the airlift. In addition, the possible evacuation of approximately 2,000 people was also discussed. Initially, a force of sixteen Dakota aircraft was authorised with the missions to be completed under Operation Knicker.

Operation Rush

At midday on 20 April 1948, a signal was sent by HQ Transport Command to HQ 46 Group, announcing that an eight-aircraft detachment would be required by HQ BAFO to mount a shuttle service between Gatwick and Bückeburg from 23 to 30 April, under Operation Rush. The operation was later reduced to four aircraft (KN330, KN607, KN381 and KN552) and the task allocated to 77 Squadron at Waterbeach along with support provided by staff from RAF Oakington. The four aircraft arrived at Bückeburg on 22 April to commence their duties. By 25 April, twenty loaded sorties had been flown and a total of 128,619 lb of freight carried. The aircraft returned to RAF Waterbeach on 25 April, via Oakington to drop off the Movements party, having flown a total of 70 hours including the outward and return journeys.

Bückeburg scheduled services

Meanwhile, the daily scheduled activities at Bückeburg were increasing, particularly in connection with the 'P.19' scheduled daily flights. Initially these had been operated by Anson aircraft shuttling people, freight and mail into and out of the British controlled areas of Berlin. However, by the beginning of May, they had been supplemented by Dakota aircraft, while the number of daily flights also increased. Using information extracted from Bückeburg's Form 540s for May 1948, a summary of their activities is shown below:

Anson	285 hours allotted	283.40 hours flown
Dakota	50 hours allotted	72.40 hours flown
Other types	135 hours allotted	103.20 hours flown

Considering the relatively short distance and flight duration, these numbers represent a high level of activity.

On 20 June 1948, in an action that showed their determination to have all of Berlin under their own control, the Soviets closed all of the road, railway and canal links from western-occupied Germany into western-occupied Berlin. This action, they believed, would make it impossible for the residents to obtain food and other supplies and would eventually drive Britain, France and the USA out of the city for good. Clearly, the Soviets underestimated the Allies. Instead of retreating from West Berlin, they decided to supply their sectors of the city from the air.

The British Government's decision, along with those of her American ally, to beat the Soviet blockade using an airborne supply route, was going to take some considerable effort. The Joint Staffs in London estimated that 4,000–5,000 tons of food, supplies and fuel were required for each day just to keep the city going.

On 24 June, RAF Waterbeach received a request for six Dakota aircraft for the Operation Knicker deployment. Just five hours later, the number had been raised to eight aircraft. The aircraft were required to be at Wünsdorf the following day. At 2210 hours on 24 June, an 'Immediate' signal message from HQ Transport Command was sent to HQ 46 Group: 'KNICKER GO AT HALF SCALE. AGREE STAFF DETACHMENT ACCOMPANY.'

This effectively authorised the start of the operation at 50 per cent of the previously agreed effort utilising eight out of sixteen aircraft.

The following information has been extracted from the Form F540s for RAF Waterbeach and illustrates how activities proceeded:

25 June: 'The first party of eight aircraft and personnel proceeded to Wunstorf on Operation Knicker.'

27 June: 'Information was received that eight aircraft and crews were required for Operation Knicker to take off between 1045 and 1130 hours on 28 June.'

28 June: 'Instructions were received that Operation Knicker was to proceed at full scale. A further party of ten aircraft and personnel proceed to Wunstorf.'

29 June: 'A further party of eight aircraft and personnel proceeded to Wunstorf on Operation Knicker now renamed Carter Paterson.'

30 June: 'Station Commander (Group Captain N.C. Hyde)... proceeded to Wunstorf on Operation Plain Fare to take charge of the transport force.'

Carter Paterson or Plain Fare?

It has been reported in some quarters that the original operational name chosen for this significantly increased level of supply activity was Carter Paterson; selected because it was named after one of London's largest removal organisations. However, the Soviets cleverly utilised this knowledge when issuing their regular broadcast of misinformation to the residents of the Allied areas of Berlin, suggesting that the British were moving all of the equipment and supplies out of Berlin, rather than into Berlin! Shortly afterwards, the operational name was changed to Plain Fare, although this has also been seen as Plane Fair in some documents. Eventually, it settled as Plainfare.

The Chief of Staff, Lord Tedder, advised his fellow Chiefs of Staff on 28 June 1948 that the RAF would be able to arrange a lift of 75 tons a day into Berlin by air immediately and that this could be raised to 400 tons a day within 48 hours. After 3 July, when the Gatow airport runway had been re-opened after repairs, this figure would rise to 750 tons a day. However, the cost was to stop all Service transport except to Berlin and Warsaw.

Clearly, achieving the required 4,000–5,000 tons per day could not be achieved by the RAF alone. Transport Command had eight Dakota and eight Avro York squadrons in the UK; although the Command was very much in crisis following the post-war budget-cap along with downsizing and demobilisation of both air and ground crews.

American support assured

Fortunately, the co-operation of the Americans was assured. In Washington, the resolve of President Truman needed no strengthening. He too was adamant that the Western Allies should maintain their presence in Berlin. Following a meeting held on 28–29 June, it was clear that the British Government could rely on US support. Initially, the United States Air Force (USAF) would add 50–100 Douglas C-54 Skymaster aircraft to the airlift. With their 10-ton lifting capacity, these were crucial to the Allies maintaining the required level of supplies.

By August 1948, the Air Ministry officially noted that the RAF was carrying an average 1,100 tons a day into Berlin, using Avro York and Douglas Dakota aircraft from Transport Command, along with flying-boats (including Sunderland aircraft) from Coastal Command. At this time, the American contribution was averaging over 1,500 tons a day with an estimated fleet of around 100 aircraft.

The problems for Transport Command were being compounded by a lack of skilled crews and the demobilisation was continuing. However, in a signal to Commanders-in-Chief on 13 August, the Air Ministry said that all flying crews who were due for Release were to be retained until further notice. Initially, Transport Command ground crews had been boosted by the loan of 300 additional technicians transferred from other Commands. Unfortunately, these had to be returned to their parent units and the requirement would later be covered by civilian maintenance contracts.

The next problem for Transport Command was the complete lack of any training available as all of their aircraft were being utilised on the airlift. It was planned to withdraw up to thirty-two aircraft from the airlift to allow the training programme to recommence. This would reduce the RAF's daily tonnage by up to 400 tons. Thankfully, the daily tonnage into Berlin would not be reduced as twenty-seven additional USAF C-54 Skymaster aircraft arrived at Fassburg on 20–22 August.

By 2 September, the following daily tonnages were being reported:

USAF (from the American Zone)	1,587 tons
USAF (from Fassburg)	682 tons
RAF	1,145 tons
Civilian contractors	101 tons
TOTAL	3,515 tons

The additional USAF activity of twenty C-54 Skymasters at Fassburg meant that twenty-five RAF Dakota aircraft from 46 Group had to be removed from this base and transferred to Lübeck. As the American build up at Fassburg continued, more Dakota aircraft were transferred to Lübeck.

Enter the civilian contractors

The question of RAF Transport Command's training requirements continued to raise its head in early September; thankfully, additional civilian contractors became available. On 10 September, the first eight civilian Dakota aircraft became available and eight similar RAF aircraft were withdrawn into the training role. A further ten civilian aircraft became available on 22 September when a further six Dakota aircraft were withdrawn, with the remaining four Avro York aircraft withdrawn soon afterwards.

Later in the month further civilian aircraft were brought into the airlift including four Dakotas, three Halifaxes, two Wayfarers (Bristol Type 170 Freighter), and one each of the Hythe flying-boat (civilian conversion of Short Sunderland), Avro Tudor and Vickers Viking.

The expansion of the fleet continued with additional USAF C-54 Skymaster aircraft along with the introduction into service of the Hastings. In September 1948, the four-engine Hastings, which carried 9.5 tons, was introduced into Transport Command and immediately added to the Berlin Airlift. The Hastings moved into Schleswigland on 1 November and conducted their first Plainfare missions on 11 November. Schleswigland was one of three new despatching bases in the British Zone, the others being Lübeck for Dakota operations and Fuhlsbuttel for British civilian aircraft. Schleswigland – opened in November 1948 – was also used by civilian carriers, as was Wunsdorf, the base for the Avro York operations.

In somewhat simplistic terms, the plan for the Airlift was that a northern corridor ran into Gatow and a southern corridor into Tempelhof. There was a 'time block' system, with every 24-hour period divided into 4-hour cycles, and landing slots were allocated to each despatching base according to the number of aircraft it had available. The weather during the winter of 1948/49 was typically dull, but unseasonably mild between December and the end of February, which fortuitously reduced the demand for heating coal. Another factor assisting the Allies was the opening of Tegel airfield in early December, built from scratch in the French Zone and providing a third Berlin terminal.

Soviet blockade fails!

By the spring of 1949, it was clear it was clear that the Soviet blockade of West Berlin had failed. Politically, it had not persuaded the residents of West Berlin to reject their allies in the west, nor had it prevented the formation of a unified West German state with the Federal Republic of Germany being established in May 1949. On 12 May 1949, the Soviet authorities lifted the blockade and reopened the roads, canals and railway routes into the western half of the city. The Allies continued the airlift into September as they wanted to stockpile supplies in Berlin just in case the Soviets changed their minds and the blockade resumed.

By 12 May 1949, more than 1.6 million tons had been delivered to Berlin, with an additional 713,000 tons being added to the figure before the airlift was officially lifted on 1 September 1949 when the Combined Airlift Task Force was disbanded.

Transport Command had had twenty squadrons and two OCUs involved in Operation Plainfare: Nos 10, 18, 27, 30, 46, 53, 62 and 77 operating Dakota aircraft; Nos 24, 40, 51, 59, 99, 206, 242 and 511 operating Avro York aircraft; Nos 47 and 297 operating the new Handley Page Hastings aircraft; Nos 201 and 230 operating Sunderland flying-boats; and Nos 240 and 241 OCU operating Dakota and York aircraft respectively.

The following statistics illustrate the overall achievements and effectiveness of the airlift. They were extracted from the 'Report on Operation Plainfare (The Berlin Airlift) 25 June 1948 – 6 October 1949', compiled by Air Marshal T. M. Williams, CB, OBE, MC, DFC in April 1950 and cover the period between 26 June 1948 and the 30 September 1949:

Total Tonnage lifted to Berlin:
British aircraft: 542,236 tons
US aircraft: 1,783,573 tons
Total   2,325,809 tons

Highest daily British tonnage: 2,314.5 tons on 5 July 1949

Highest daily RAF tonnage: 1,735.6 tons on 17 August 1948

Total return trips to Berlin:
By US aircraft: 379,688
By British aircraft: 175,682
Total: 525,370

Hours flown to and from Berlin:
US Aircraft: 589,524 hours
British Aircraft: 193,249
Total: 782,773

Miles flown to and from Berlin:

US Aircraft:	73,500,000 miles (estimated)
British Aircraft:	30,858,951 miles
Total:	104,358,951 miles

Many historians consider that the Soviet blockade of Berlin was a political failure for a number of reasons. It significantly increased Cold War tensions while ensuring the USSR looked to the rest of the world like a cruel and capricious enemy. Despite the Soviets' best intentions it hastened the creation of West Germany and, by demonstrating that the US and European nations had common interests as well as a common foe, it fuelled the ideas for the creation of the North Atlantic Treaty Organisation (NATO).

In the end it was transport aircraft which won a notable victory and the RAF Transport Command force which helped to sustain Britain's position in the alliance – along with delivering 23 per cent of the total tonnage.

OPERATING ROUTES OF THE AIRLIFT

(This chart should be studied in conjunction with the Altitude Separation Chart on page 23.)

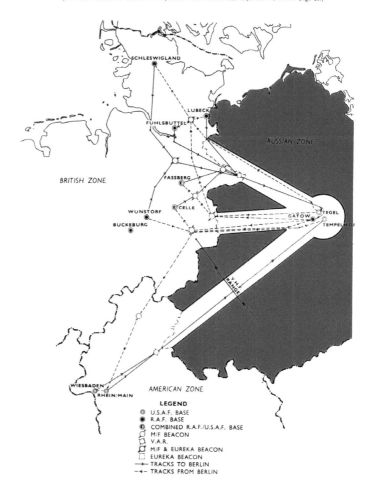

A diagram showing the Operational Routes used by the Allies to get aircraft into and out of Berlin during Operation Plainfare. (*Crown Copyright/Air Historical Branch AP-3257-Op-PlainfareReport-AirCorridors*)

43

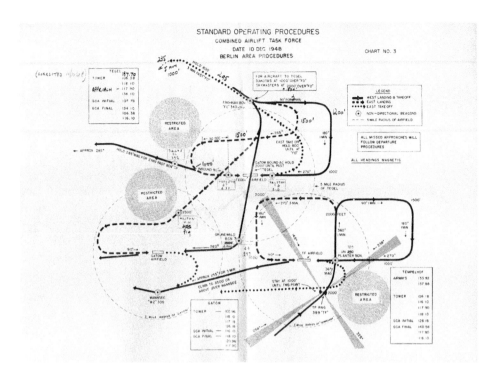

For the flight crews the journey into and out of Berlin was particularly difficult, as this Instrument Flying Chart ably demonstrates, especially when one considers the limited navigation aids at the time. (*Crown Copyright/Air Historical BranchF540-Gatow-0349-SOPs-1*)

Handley Page Hastings transport aircraft parked on the partially completed hardstandings at Schleswigland airfield, Germany, on 22 November 1948 as German labourers continue to work in the foreground. (*Crown Copyright/Air Historical Branch R-2044*)

One of the many Avro York aircraft being unloaded at Gatow. (*Crown Copyright/Air Historical Branch H-4195*)

During the airlift, there were multiple examples of undercarriage failures from aircraft swinging off the runway upon landing. Here, an unidentified Avro York is being examined after such an incident. (*Crown Copyright/Air Historical Branch H-4196*)

Aircraft from all units across Transport Command were pressed into service for Operation Plainfare. Here, Avro York C.1, MW315, of the Transport Command Examination Unit is refuelled at Wunstorf airfield during September 1948. (*Crown Copyright/Air Historical Branch R-1789*)

A view of some of the stores being held in a hangar, thought to be at Wunstorf, waiting to be loaded on to the aircraft bound for Berlin, during September 1948. (*Crown Copyright/Air Historical Branch R-1795*)

A pair of Avro York aircraft (MW302/AK and MW105) leads an Avro Tudor transport as they taxy out at Wunstorf, bound for Gatow, during Operation Plainfare in September 1948. (*Crown Copyright/Air Historical Branch R-1797*)

Ground crew completing the all-important aircraft documentation at Wunstof in September 1948. (*Crown Copyright/Air Historical Branch R-1811*)

After a wave of York aircraft had landed, they were marshalled in front of the hangars, allowing the German labourers to start the unloading process. In the front is York C.1 MW287/KY-N of 242 Squadron with similar York C.1 aircraft MW286 and MW303 parked nearby in this image taken at Gatow on 16 September 1948. (*Crown Copyright/Air Historical Branch R-1818*)

Clearly Operation Plainfare was a round-the-clock operation as this image, taken later that evening, with York C.1 MW105/YY-A of 241 OCU at the front of the line, shows to good effect. (*Crown Copyright/Air Historical Branch R-1821*)

47

British and American air crews monitor the daily flying board to see how the Berlin Airlift is proceeding during September 1948 again. (*Crown Copyright/Air Historical Branch R-1852*)

Bags of coal awaiting collection. During Operation Plainfare supplies were stockpiled on the airfield in case the rail links failed. (*Crown Copyright/Air Historical Branch H-4170*)

German workers loading coal from a 10-ton Hanomag truck onto a waiting Hastings C.1 at Schleswingland on 22 November 1948. Once the process was finished a member of the ground loading party checked the loading before the weight of the cargo was entered onto the aircraft manifest. (*Crown Copyright/Air Historical Branch R-2045*)

Nothing could be wasted! German female workers carefully collect the sweepings of coal from beneath the cargo door of a USAF C-54 Skymaster after it had been unloaded at Gatow in September 1948. (*Crown Copyright/Air Historical Branch R-1825*)

Short Sunderland V, VB389/NS-D, of 201 Squadron after landing at Havel Lake in September 1948, with its contents being loaded onto barges. The tonnage carried by the flying boats was relatively small but the Berliners were impressed with their contribution. The Sunderland aircraft continued to operate in Operation Plainfare until December 1948, by which time the airlift by land-based aircraft into Berlin's airfields had increased considerably. (*Crown Copyright/Air Historical Branch R-1831*)

The first Hastings C.1 (TG526 of 47 Squadron) to land at Schleswigland, photographed just before touchdown on 22 November 1948. (*Crown Copyright/Air Historical Branch R-2050*)

The crew relax on the wing of the very first Dakota aircraft that flew supplies into Gatow on 26 June 1948. (*Crown Copyright/Air Historical Branch H-4204*)

Korea, Malaya and the 'Japan Shuttle' (1950–54)

The Coronation Review of the Royal Air Force by HM Queen Elizabeth II at RAF Odiham on 15 July 1953. The culmination of seven months of careful planning can be seen in this aerial view of the immaculately parked aircraft and their crews as they wait in the afternoon sun for the Queen to inspect them. Two Transport Command Hastings aircraft were prominently located. (*Crown Copyright/Air Historical Branch AHB-UNK-CoronationReview-Colour-12*)

A significant contribution to the Second World War was shortly followed by the Berlin Airlift. During both, Transport Command had demonstrated its value and ability many times over. However, they were now entering a further period of peace and financial retrenchment following the massive costs of both. Basically, the UK could no longer afford to keep a worldwide transport authority in place, particularly when an emphasis was being placed on a nuclear deterrent force.

Despite everyone's best efforts at peace, Britain was heavily committed in Malaya where Operation Firedog, a civil and military campaign aimed at isolating the communist insurgents, was under way. It was a conflict that was destined to run until 1960.

Cutting the home forces

The Statement on Defence for 1950 stated bluntly that 'with the gradual build-up of Bomber Command there will be a reduction in the air transport force at home'. The immediate implications meant the abolishment of both 46 and 38 Groups, effectively removing the intermediate layer altogether and leaving Transport Command HQ to assume direct responsibility for transport squadrons in the UK.

Before the end of January 1950, instructions had been issued to the Command to disband four medium-range squadrons, and for one of its remaining two medium-range squadrons to take over the role of the Transport Support Training Unit. The squadrons to be disbanded during February were Nos 10, 18, 46 and 206; No. 207 personnel were to be posted and the squadron number-plate transferred to the Training Unit, which was to be reorganised and provisionally located at Abingdon. Meanwhile, 24 Squadron was to be reduced to five or six long-range and three or four medium-range aircraft.

The status of Transport Command on 31 January 1951 was just four squadrons of Hastings – two at Topcliffe (Nos 47 and 53) and two at Lyneham (Nos 99 and 511), all in the long-range role; a Hastings/York Special squadron at Lyneham (No. 24 (Commonwealth)); a Dakota/Valetta squadron at Abingdon (No. 30) in the medium-range role; and a communications squadron at Hendon with an assortment of types – Anson, Devon, Proctor, and a single Spitfire LF.16. Transport Command had an authorised total of 166 aircraft, with 186 actually on hand.

In 1951, the Government statements were slightly less pessimistic and a little later, a Memorandum by the Secretary of State for Air to accompany the 1951–52 Air Estimates, advised that the 'rundown of Transport Command had been halted'.

'Japan Shuttle'

Successive Statements on Defence reflected the variety of ways in which the Command was called on 'to support British policy' in unsettled times. They also identified that the Hastings aircraft had become the workhorse of the Command in the early 1950s. These events included the Hastings running a casualty evacuation service carrying wounded soldiers of the UN forces from Korea. In October 1952, at very short notice and without mishap, Transport Command accomplished the task of carrying large formations of British troops to the Middle East.

The Korean evacuation flights became known as the 'Japan Shuttle'. In late 1950, Transport Command undertook a number of special flights to Japan in support of British Forces in Korea. On the return flights, the aircraft continued to be used for casualty evacuation to the UK – although these included Turkish Army personnel who were flown as far as Habbaniyah. By early 1951, these journeys became 'routine' when a once-weekly Singapore–Japan service was inaugurated in February 1951 utilising Hastings aircraft. Once again, the return flight was used for casualties, but in addition to British personnel, it now carried Turkish, Greek, Dutch, Belgian, Indian and French casualties. Based at RAF Topcliffe, the duties were conducted by aircraft and crews from 47 Squadron.

In addition to the Korean commitment, there was an even larger task looming as a result of the need to position crews and aircraft at Fayid, Egypt, owing to the international crisis which had blown up following the Persian intention to nationalise the Abadan oil refineries.

Troubles in Cyprus

Then, a yet bigger Middle East commitment occurred: moving Army personnel from the UK to Castel Benito, Tripoli, and from there – and also from Nicosia, Cyprus – to Fayid. An Operational Record Book entry confirmed that this operation lasted for twenty-two days, when 5,342 troops and 362,350 lb of freight were uplifted without incident.

Transport Command was being stretched to its limits – and beyond. For 47 Squadron, based at RAF Topcliffe, they had no aircraft available for flying in the UK for twelve days as a direct result of detachments to the Middle and Far East.

Meanwhile, the Blackburn Beverly, a development of the General Aircraft Limited GAL 60 Universal transport aircraft, made its first flight in 1950. It was the largest aircraft ever manufactured in the UK and had been designed ahead of GAL's merger with Blackburn in 1946. The prototype, WL320, made an appearance at the SBAC show at Farnborough in September 1951. A total of forty-seven were eventually ordered for the RAF but they did not enter service until 1956. At least Transport Command had something positive on the horizon.

Becher's Brook

The end of the Second World War did not end the requirement for Transport Command's Ferry Unit. On 2 January 1953, the first batch of Canadair-built Sabre F.1 and F.4 aircraft for the RAF were handed over during a ceremony at RAF Abingdon by Mr Norman Robertson, the Canadian High Commissioner, to the Secretary of State for Air, the Lord de L'Isle and Dudley VC. The aircraft had been ferried from Canada to the UK by pilots of the Transport Command Overseas Ferry Unit (later 147 Squadron) in Operation Becher's Brook, which lasted from 8 December 1952 to 19 December 1953.

The Sabre was the RAF's first swept-wing fighter and was acquired as a stop-gap measure to equip the RAF with a fighter in the 700 mph class until the Hawker Hunter could enter service; which it eventually did in the spring of 1955. In total 430 Sabre F.1 and F.4 aircraft were acquired under the Mutual Aid Programme.

The 3,100-mile delivery flights via Goose Bay, Greenland, Iceland and Prestwick, could take anything from two days to three weeks depending on the weather. All were flown by specially trained crews from 147 Squadron.

Coronation Review

The Coronation Review of the Royal Air Force by HM the Queen was held at RAF Odiham in July 1953. The event was an enormous test of the RAF's planning and culminated with more than 300 aircraft available for inspection by HM the Queen on the ground, followed by a flypast led by one helicopter and containing 640 aircraft, of which 440 were jet-powered. The flypast ran with absolute precision.

RAF Transport Command was represented on the ground with both Hasting and Valetta aircraft in the static display; while six Valetta aircraft and three Hastings aircraft were included in the massed formations.

Order placed for Comet C.2

The de Havilland Comet, the world's first turbojet transport, had not enjoyed an easy entry into airline service and its problems have been well documented. On 27 August 1953 the Comet 2, with its heavier gauge fuselage skin and round windows, made its first flight from Hatfield. Although initial trials showed the aircraft to be unsuitable for the North Atlantic crossing, an order was eventually placed to acquire up to fifteen aircraft for use with Transport Command's 216 Squadron. Deliveries did not commence until 1956.

However, the order for the Comet 2 had been placed against the background of the Vickers V1000, an aircraft identified by Operational Requirement 315 (OR315) for a pure jet passenger/freighter to replace the Hastings in long-range service with Transport Command. An initial proposal for twenty-four V1000 aircraft to work alongside thirty-two Beverley aircraft was seen to meet the forward Air Mobility requirements. This proposal was later arbitrarily reduced to twelve V1000 and twenty-four Beverley aircraft to meet Ministry of Defence cost-cutting requirements.

Around the same time, the proposed Bristol Britannia was also under consideration in the long-range passenger/transport role. Unfortunately, the V1000 would not be available until 1958, so the stop-gap order for the Comet C.2 was placed.

The V1000 continued to be the vehicle of choice for Transport Command but its forecast performance was falling behind the operational requirement and the in-service date had slipped to 1960. Interesting times were ahead.

Members of the Argyll and Sutherland Highlanders boarding the first Transport Command Hastings aircraft to leave RAF Lyneham for Japan, on 19 September 1950. The troops were reinforcements for British forces in Korea. (*Crown Copyright/Air Historical Branch PRB-1-931*)

WF320, the prototype Blackburn and General Aircraft Universal Freighter, displaying at the 1951 SBAC Show at Farnborough, held between 11 and 16 September. Despite its bulky appearance, the aircraft impressed onlookers with its impressive take-off and landing capabilities; as well as its ability to taxi backwards on the runway. The Universal Freighter was developed into the Beverley for use by the RAF, with deliveries to Transport Command squadrons commencing in 1956. (*Crown Copyright/Air Historical Branch PRB-1-3377*)

Following the decision by Egypt in October 1951 to terminate the 1936 Anglo-Egyptian Treaty, RAF Transport Command undertook a round-the-clock operation to fly 3,500 British reinforcements into the Canal Zone. Four Transport Command Hastings aircraft, including TG562, were photographed on the ramp at Nicosia on 1 November 1951. (*Crown Copyright/Air Historical Branch CMP-228*)

The first of four Hastings C.4 VIP transports, WD500, posed for a publicity shot at RAF Topcliffe in December 1951. The richly appointed cabin had a combined dining and conference room which doubled up as sleeping quarters for overnight flights, rear-facing leather seats and strip lighting, which could be dimmed. Despite all of this apparent luxury, the passengers may occasionally have felt some discomfort in the unpressurised cabin. WD500 was originally delivered as a C.2 variant to the A&AEE at Boscombe Down on 1 October 1951 before joining 24 Squadron at Topcliffe on 19 October. It was returned to Handley Page for modifications on 16 September 1952 when it re-emerged at the first C.4 VIP aircraft on 16 October before subsequently rejoining 24 Squadron. (*Crown Copyright/Air Historical Branch PRB-1-3973*)

Airmen check the external mounting points under the forward fuselage of a Handley Page Hastings temporarily flying with a Parachute Training Unit in Egypt. The aircraft has been loaded with two jeeps which were to be dropped by parachute during a training exercise with Army troops on 4 February 1952. A line of unidentified late-model Spitfires can be seen in the distance under the wing of the Hastings. (*Crown Copyright/Air Historical Branch CMP-500*)

Paratroops of the 16th Independent Parachute Group jumping from Handley Page Hastings C.1 TG508/A during a demonstration drop in the Canal Zone on 4 February 1952. The aircraft is also carrying a Land Rover and 75 mm howitzer in special external carriers under the forward fuselage. The aircraft is from the Station Flight at RAF Abingdon. (*Crown Copyright/ Air Historical Branch CMP-498*)

Engine fitters working on one of the propellers of Avro York C.1 WW502 after it landed at Fayid, Egypt, on 8 April 1952. Some sources indicate that the serial WW502 is in a batch 'used temporarily for civilian Avro York aircraft flying into the Canal Zone under treaty'. The civilian registration of the aircraft is known to be G-AHFH. (*Crown Copyright/Air Historical Branch CMP-525*)

A line of twenty-eight Canadair Sabre F.4s sitting at Goose Bay, Labrador, during one of the numerous ferry flights undertaken between Canada and the UK as part of Operation Becher's Brook. The 3,100-mile flights via Goose Bay, Greenland, Iceland and Prestwick could take anything from two days to three weeks depending on the weather. All were flown by specially trained crews from 147 Squadron of Transport Command. (*Crown Copyright/Air Historical Branch PRB-1-7033*)

The crew of Hastings C.2 WJ327 take the opportunity to view one of five nine-aircraft formations of Avro Lincolns drawn from Bomber Command as they fly over the parade 1,200 feet above the airfield during the Coronation Review at RAF Odiham on 15 July 1953. *(Crown Copyright/Air Historical Branch X-46567)*

Having displayed the prototype 'Universal Transport' at the previous year's SBAC Air Show, Blackburn displayed the second prototype, now known as the Beverley C.1, at the 1953 event. The aircraft, WZ889, waits at the end of Farnborough's runway to commence its flying display. (*Crown Copyright/Air Historical Branch PRB-1-6848a*)

Transport Command activities at RAF Lyneham in 1954, with a Hastings C.2 (WJ338/GAC) and Valetta C.1 (VL280) photographed while flying in formation on 8 April 1954. The letters 'GAC' worn by the Hastings refer to the aircraft's radio call sign. Valetta C.1 VL280 operated with a variety of units including the Ferry Training Unit as well as 167 Squadron at RAF Benson. (*Crown Copyright/ Air Historical Branch PRB-1-7608*)

Vickers Valetta C.1 VW842 of 30 Squadron taking off from RAF Northolt at the start of the weekly diplomatic mail service to Warsaw on 13 July 1954. (*Crown Copyright/Air Historical Branch PRB-1-8429*)

Entering the Jet Transport Age (1955–59)

De Havilland Comet C.2 XK697 from 216 Squadron at RAF Lyneham in September 1957. It was during this month that the squadron commenced regular flights to Christmas Island in the Pacific where a base had been built to carry out the first drop of a British-built thermonuclear weapon (H-Bomb). The route took in stops at Keflavik (Iceland), Goose Bay (Canada), Offutt Air Force Base (Nebraska), Travis AFB (California), Honolulu (Hawaii) and on to Christmas Island. (*Crown Copyright/Air Historical Branch T-513*)

It was becoming clear that the forecast performance of the V1000 was dropping below the operational requirement. Weight growth without a matching increase in engine thrust was causing the aircraft to be underpowered. It also meant that the use of 6,000-foot runways would impose serious payload limitations, which would in turn prevent the aircraft providing the required range and payload.

It came as no surprise to many that, following a meeting on 27 July 1955, the Air Council cancelled the order for the V1000 and recommended an order for the Britannia instead. The future for Transport Command's long-range force would consist of Britannia C.1 aircraft supported by Comet C.2 aircraft. For some, placing the order for the Britannia was seen as a blatant political move in an effort to win votes; a number of the aircraft were to be built by Short Brothers at Belfast – then an unemployment black spot!

Blackburn and Comet enters service

In March 1956, the first Beverley C.1 was delivered to 47 Squadron at RAF Abingdon. Among the Beverley's first tasks was the delivery of Sycamore and Whirlwind helicopters to Cyprus.

RAF Transport Command eventually took delivery of fifteen Comets, beginning with XK670, which was 'officially' delivered to RAF Lyneham on 7 July 1956, although this aircraft was actually used for a VIP flight almost two weeks ahead of this date. XK670, along with XK669, were originally designated Comet T.2s and employed for crew training. Subsequently, 216 Squadron received eight Comet C.2s equipped as normal transport aircraft. Later, both T.2 variants were converted back to C.2 airframes and returned to the squadron at Lyneham to complete the ten-aircraft compliment.

216 Squadron's Comet aircraft had a significant impact on Transport Command's long-range abilities, bringing the most distant parts of the Commonwealth within less than two days' travelling from the UK, and the Far East inside 24 hours.

Interestingly, 216 Squadron's first operational flight with the new type had been to fly the Secretary of State for Air (Rt Hon Nigel Birch) to Moscow on 23 June 1956 for the Russian Air Display at Vhukovo. A number of invited guests were also onboard for the trip. The 1,490-mile flight took just 4 hours and 2 minutes.

Suez Crisis

Back in October 1954, Egypt abrogated the treaty whereby the British Army and the RAF were permitted bases in the Canal Zone until 1956, with the possibility of extension beyond that date by negotiation. Withdrawal of equipment began to bases in both Cyprus and Aden, which were to become the major centres of the British military presence in the Middle East. In the summer of 1956, just three months after the British withdrawal had been completed, a major crisis broke.

On 26 July 1956, President Nasser of Egypt announced the nationalisation of the Suez Canal Company. This was in retaliation for the British and US Governments reneging on an agreement for the financing of the Aswan Dam project. The Suez Canal represented the main source of supply of oil for both Britain and France and the potential loss of those supplies represented an economic threat that they could not ignore. In addition, there was a significant increase in military aid for Egypt from the Communist Bloc.

The Anglo-French sea-borne invasion, supported by parachute forces to occupy the Canal Zone, was launched from Malta and Cyprus under the name Operation Musketeer. The RAF was to play a significant role in the mission. For Transport Command, 30 Squadron at RAF Dishforth operating Valetta C.1 aircraft and numbers 90 and 511 Squadrons operating Hastings C.1 aircraft all participated in troop and parachute flights, most of which were flown out of Cyprus. By November 1956, a ceasefire had been declared and all French and British troops were withdrawn from the region and replaced by a UN peacekeeping force.

AWRE in Australia

In 1956, the main workhorse of Transport Command was the venerable Hastings. At the time, the Atomic Weapons Research Establishment (AWRE) were testing weapons in Australia and required eleven special flights to Australia along with a detachment of three or four Hastings in that country to support their operations. There was also a requirement to continue six return flights per month to Australia in support of further guided weapons development. It provided yet another stress on Transport Command's limited assets.

Following the outstanding success of the single-engine Pioneer in service with the RAF at home and overseas there was a decision in 1956 to order the larger twin-engine aircraft from the same manufacturer. The initial order for the RAF was for twenty Twin Pioneer CC.1 aircraft and the first military variant made its first flight on 29 August 1957. The contract was increased initially to thirty-two aircraft, and later up to thirty-nine; the last seven of which were designated CC.2 aircraft. Deliveries to the RAF began in early 1958 and were all delivered by March 1961.

21 Squadron were re-formed at RAF Benson on 1 March 1959 and took delivery of a number of Pioneer CC.1 aircraft, although their time in the UK was relatively short-lived as the squadron was transferred to Eastleigh, Kenya, in September of the same year.

Emergency aid for Hungary

In October 1956, following an unsuccessful uprising by the Hungarians against the occupying Soviet forces, Valetta C.1 aircraft of 30 Squadron, normally based at RAF Dishforth, flew emergency aid and medical supplies from RAF Wildenrath, Germany, into Vienna to provide assistance for around 100,000 Hungarian refugees who had escaped the Red Army by moving across the border into Austria. A total fleet of twenty-one aircraft (including Transport Command Hastings and Beverley C.1 aircraft) eventually flew a combined load of 112 tons of aid on behalf of the Red Cross.

King Hussein requests assistance

From 1955, the Soviet Union had provided military aid to both Egypt and Syria, including the supply of aircraft and the building of airfields in Syria. These airfields, located to the west of Syria, clearly threatened Lebanese and Jordanian integrity. In February 1958, the United Arab Republic (UAR) was formed between Egypt and Syria. Simultaneously, Iraq and Jordan agreed to an anti-communist, anti-Nasser Federation. The tension at the eastern end of the Mediterranean grew with a revolt in Lebanon and, following the assassination of the Iraqi president, King Hussein of Jordan appealed to Britain on 16 July for assistance in maintaining stability.

The request was immediately supported and on the following morning 200 troops were moved to Amman from Cyprus by Hastings aircraft of 70 Squadron. For a time they seemed to be isolated, since Israel temporarily refused permission for further overflights. After pressure from the US Government, Israel relented and successive flights of RAF transport aircraft were escorted by US Navy fighters from the Sixth Fleet.

By 18 July, 2,200 troops were in Amman with light artillery support. Reinforcements had been flown into Cyprus by Comet C.2s of Transport Command's 216 Squadron, assisted by Shackleton aircraft drawn from 42 and 204 Squadron. Meanwhile Beverley C.1 aircraft (including a number from Transport Command squadrons) flew in heavy equipment from Cyprus. The troops were followed by a detachment of Hunter F.6 aircraft from 208 Squadron on 20 July from Akrotiri.

King Hussein established a pledge of loyalty from the powerful Bedouin tribes on 11 August and British troops began withdrawing after a UN resolution called for an end to Western intervention later in the month. The last British troops left on 2 November 1958.

Belvedere HC.1 ordered

The Belvedere HC.1 was the first twin-engine, twin-rotor helicopter to enter service with the RAF. An order was initially placed for twenty-six Belvederes and the first RAF machine (XG447) made its first flight on 5 July 1958. The Belvedere was designed to meet the RAF's requirements for troop and freight transport, paratrooping, supply-dropping, casualty evacuation, and any other kind of requirement associated with Army cooperation activities. In September 1959, one of the first pre-production machines (XG461) gave a spectacular performance of its capabilities at the SBAC Show at Farnborough, including operating with a dummy Bloodhound surface-to-air missile under-slung during the display.

Britannia enters service

The introduction of the Bristol Britannia provided Transport Command with its first turboprop transport aircraft, and the type subsequently operated widely on long-range strategic missions in many parts of the world, forming the basis for the rapid deployment of the Army's United Kingdom Strategic Reserve.

The circumstance surrounding the initial order for six Britannia C.1 aircraft has been discussed above. The initial order was later increased to ten and finally to twenty-three aircraft. The first Britannia C.1 (XL635) made its first flight at Belfast on 29 December 1958 with the last aircraft being delivered to the RAF on 2 December 1960.

The first unit to receive the new turboprop design was 99 Squadron, who took delivery of a number of Britannia C.1 aircraft in March 1959, while trading-in their former Hastings C.1 and C.2 mounts around the same time. Later, in December 1959, 99 Squadron was followed by 511 Squadron; with both units operating the Britannia from RAF Lyneham.

By the end of 1959, Transport Command operated as a self-contained formation, without Groups – unlike both Bomber and Fighter Command. However, all of the Comet C.2 aircraft were all now in service and performing well. The Britannia was on the horizon but the Command still needed to replace thirty Beverley C.1 aircraft, along with thirty-two Hastings. Two types were required: a long-range strategic freighter to replace the Hastings and a medium-range tactical freighter to supplement and eventually replace the Beverley. Final decisions would eventually be made on both requirements.

A Hastings C.4 VIP transport aircraft (WJ324) of 24 Squadron at RAF Northolt, photographed on 30 June 1955. (*Crown Copyright/Air Historical Branch PRB-1-10060*)

The 216 Squadron crew which took the Secretary of State for Air, the Rt Hon Nigel Birch MP, to Moscow on 23 June 1956 aboard Comet C.2 XK670. (*Crown Copyright/ Air Historical Branch PRB-1-11874*)

The Rt Hon Nigel Birch MP, Secretary of State for Air (right), talks with Colonel Konstantinov, the Russian Air Attaché in London, before they board Comet C.2 (XK670) of 216 Squadron in which they flew to Moscow. (*Crown Copyright/ Air Historical Branch PRB-1-11888*)

A copy of the 216 Squadron visitors book for the historic flight of Comet C.2 XK670 to Moscow on 23 June 1956. (*Crown Copyright/Air Historical Branch AHB-216sqn-visitorsbook*)

Vickers Valetta C.1 aircraft (including VW201) of 30 Squadron being loaded with emergency aid and medical supplies for Hungary at RAF Wildenrath in October 1956. The aircraft, normally based at RAF Dishforth, were part of a twenty-one-strong fleet which flew 72 of a combined 112 tons of aid into Vienna for onward shipment to Hungary by the Red Cross, following the unsuccessful uprising against the Soviet Union. (*Crown Copyright/Air Historical Branch CLP-245*)

Jeeps and trailers being loaded onto a 53 Squadron Blackburn Beverley C1, XB287/T at RAF Abingdon in the summer of 1956. The equipment was being airlifted from the UK to join the Internal Security Flight based in Cyprus. (*Crown Copyright/Air Historical Branch T-295*)

De Havilland Devon C.1, VP958, of the Metropolitan Communications Squadron based at RAF Hendon flying over Greenwich in March 1957, with the Docklands area of London below. (*Crown Copyright/Air Historical Branch PRB-1-13174*)

An early colour image of Blackburn Beverley C.1 XB284/H. At the time of its introduction into RAF service in March 1956, the Beverley was not only the largest aircraft to enter RAF service, but also the first designed for the dropping of heavy Army equipment through rear loading doors, which could be removed for this purpose – as they had been in this view. (*Crown Copyright/Air Historical Branch T-429*)

Hastings C.1 TG551/GAN wearing the colours of 99 Squadron, RAF Lyneham, in September 1957. 99 Squadron equipped with the Hasting C.1 and C.2 back in August 1949 and continued to operate the type until June 1959 when they were replaced by the Bristol Britannia C.1 and C.2. The large 'GAN' letters on the side of the fuselage are the aircraft's VHF radio call-sign. (*Crown Copyright/Air Historical Branch T-474*)

It wasn't long before the Comet C.2 was supplementing the venerable Hasting on support duties with the AWRE activities at Woomera. XK715 *Columba* and its crew were photographed at Edinburgh Field, Salisbury, South Australia. Behind is a RAAF Bristol 170 Freighter, serial A81-4. (*BAE SYSTEMS negative NK-2028*)

Devon C.2 VP958 of Transport Command's Metropolitan Communications Squadron flying over its RAF Hendon base just ahead of the airfield closure in November 1957. (*BAE SYSTEMS*)

An Avro Anson C.19 of the Metropolitan Communication Squadron taking off from Hendon on 7 November 1957. On this day, the airfield ceased flying activities after forty years and the Anson was the very last aircraft to leave the runway ahead of the base's formal closure. (*Crown Copyright/ Air Historical Branch PRB-1-14103*)

Transport Command Valetta C.1, VL280, while serving with 167 Squadron at RAF Benson in 1957. (*Crown Copyright/Air Historical Branch T-14*)

A Transport Command Beverley C.1 (foreground) and Hastings aircraft (including C.1 TG612 and C.2 WD487) at Nicosia, Cyprus, during the airlift of British forces to Jordan in July 1958. (*Crown Copyright/ Air Historical Branch CMP-971*)

A Handley Page Hastings C.1 operating with 36 Squadron (but still wearing the markings of 511 Squadron) taxies into position at Amman, Transjordan, in October 1958. (*Crown Copyright/ Air Historical Branch T-725*)

Following a UN resolution calling for the end of Western intervention in August 1958, British forces were withdrawn from Jordan. A Jordanian officer watches a Transport Command Beverley C.1 (probably from 84 Squadron) at Amman to collect another load of troops and equipment. On the left are Hunters from 208 Squadron, and in the background is a Hastings of 70 Squadron. The last British troops left on 2 November 1958. (*Crown Copyright/Air Historical Branch CMP-1014*)

Blackburn Beverley C.1, XB265/A, of 47/53 Squadron at RAF Abingdon in 1958. (*Crown Copyright/Air Historical BranchT-257*)

Parked alongside the Beverley was a Scottish Aviation Pioneer CC.1, XL557, of 215 Squadron. (*Crown Copyright/Air Historical Branch T-260*)

Towards the end of 1958, six Whirlwind HAR.2 helicopters were sent from the UK to Cyprus to provide additional rotary support for 284 Squadron during a period of increased security following a resumption of the insurgency by EOKA nationalists. The Whirlwinds, from the Joint Experimental Helicopter Unit based at Middle Wallop, were flown out on Beverley aircraft (C.1 XB268 here) of Transport Command to conduct internal security patrols over the island. One of the helicopters, XK968, was photographed being unloaded after arrival at Nicosia. (*Crown Copyright/Air Historical Branch CMP-1040*)

21 Squadron Twin
Pioneer CC.1, XM958,
photographed during a
flight from RAF Benson
in June 1959, shortly after
the squadron had officially
reformed on 1 May 1959.
(*Crown Copyright/Air
Historical Branch T-966*)

By the end of the 1950s,
the Comet C.2 and
Britannia C.1 were at the
forefront of Transport
Command operations.
Photographed on 9 June
1959 was Comet C.2
XK670 of 216 Squadron,
leading Britannia C.1
XL636 operated by both
99 and 511 Squadron – all
three squadrons resident
at RAF Lyneham. (*Crown
Copyright/Air Historical
Branch PRB-1-16809*)

An early pre-production
Bristol Belvedere HC.1,
XG451, lifting a dummy
Bloodhound surface-to-air
missile during a display
at the 1959 SBAC Show
at Farnborough. The first
operational unit of the
RAF to be equipped with
the Belvedere was 66
Squadron at RAF Odiham,
which took delivery of the
first airframe in September
1961. (*Crown Copyright/Air
Historical Branch T-1215*)

President Dwight D. Eisenhower arriving at RAF Benson on 29 September 1959, after returning from a visit to Balmoral. The President had flown in Comet C.2 XK715, named *Columba*, of 216 Squadron. (*Crown Copyright/Air Historical Branch PRB-1-17641*)

Bristol Britannia C.1, XL636 *Argo*, of 99 Squadron photographed during a flight from Lyneham in 1959. The Royal Air Force ordered a total of twenty-three Britannia aircraft and the first (XL635) made its first flight on 29 December 1958. Initially, deliveries were made to 99 Squadron in March 1959 where they replaced Hastings aircraft in service, and later to 511 Squadron. (*Crown Copyright/ Air Historical Branch T-1078*)

Air Mobility (1960–64)

Hawker Hunter F.6, XF523/N, of 54 Squadron, based at RAF Waterbeach, photographed in March 1963 carrying eight 60 lb rocket projectiles. At the time of the image, 54 Squadron was part of 38 Group, within Transport Command. (*Crown Copyright/Air Historical Branch T-3690*)

It was during the 1960s that Transport Command acquired its greatest strengths at both ends of the operational scale – a strategic airlift capability along with a tactical transport role in support of the Army.

At the end of 1959, the Air Council had considered the implications of two squadrons (Nos 99 and 511, both at RAF Lyneham) of Britannia C.1 aircraft. With the introduction of the type into the first squadron (No. 99) in March 1959, the carriage of all high-priority RAF freight would be undertaken by Transport Command. On the introduction of the second squadron (No. 511), the resultant surplus routine capacity was made available to all three Services.

Production of the first twenty Armstrong Whitworth Argosy C.1 aircraft were in production with Hawker Siddeley, ordered as a replacement for the ageing Valetta. Meanwhile, Treasury approval was being sought for a further twenty. Eventually, a total of fifty-six Argosy C.1 aircraft were built for and delivered to the RAF.

At an Air Council meeting on 4 April 1960, a replacement for the Comet C.2 was discussed. The Council agreed that five Comet C.2s should be reconditioned, three to replace aircraft in Signals Command and the other two to replace the VIP Hastings serving the Air Forces Arabian Peninsula and Far East Air Force. At the same meeting, the question of what would replace the Comet C.2 in Transport Command service was resolved when the Council recommended ordering five Comet C.4 aircraft, along with the first batch of five VC10 C.1 aircraft.

During the 1960s, the emphasis in Defence planning was on air mobility, which required Transport Command carrying the Army into its operational theatres, and supporting it along with RAF squadrons on long-range deployments. The Indonesian Confrontation of 1963–66 provides a perfect example of how long-range logistics was able to support the many bomber squadrons – of Victor, Vulcan and Canberra aircraft – sent on detachment from the UK, Germany and Cyprus in support of the Far East Air Force. Here, Transport Command Comet and Britannia aircraft carried technical and support personnel, along with the all-important spares.

38 Group and Starlight

In January 1960, 38 Group was set-up within Transport Command. Its first major strategic task was the detailed planning and execution of Exercise Starlight in March 1960. The exercise was held to test the deployment of the air-portable strategic reserve from the UK to an 'undeveloped country' and the maintenance of air support during the period of operations. The aggressor was a 'middle-eastern country with modern weapons, including tanks'. The strategic airhead was at El Adem, and by the end of the exercise the brigade airhead had moved forward some 60 miles to Tmimi with the ground forces a further 50 miles beyond that (at the limit of air supply by Beverley aircraft). A total of 3,550 personnel, 670 vehicles and trailers, 40 guns and almost 900 tons of cargo were moved through Tmimi. The RAF forces involved were Britannia aircraft of 99 Squadron; twelve Beverley aircraft of numbers 47 and 53 Squadrons; and four Hastings aircraft, all providing strategic airlift; with eight Pioneers from 230 Squadron and twelve Whirlwind helicopters from 225 Squadron operating short-range air supply flights in-theatre.

Not all of the tasks could be planned to the same extent as Starlight was. Very often, Transport Command was called upon to assist with natural disasters, all over the globe. Early in 1961, the RAF brought relief to tribesmen in the northern provinces of Kenya where serious famine had resulted from failure of the rains the previous year. In Operation Maize Bag detachments of Beverley aircraft from numbers 47, 50 and 30 Squadrons flew thirty-one sorties dropping over 300,000 lb of maize, 20,000 lb of dried meat and 2,000 lb of dried milk. The supplies were dropped in 100-lb containers, in an area virtually inaccessible to overland transport.

Ironically, in the autumn of the same year, RAF transport aircraft from the UK and the Middle East Air Force were again called upon to help Kenyan Africans, now cut off by floods. Known as Operation Tana Flood and later extended into Somalia, almost 2,700 tons of food was dropped from the air. The RAF element also involved Twin Pioneer aircraft of the locally based 21 Squadron along with Valetta C.1 aircraft of 233 Squadron.

Enter the Belvedere

The first operational unit to receive the Belvedere HC.1 was 66 Squadron at RAF Odiham, which accepted delivery of the first machine on 15 September 1961. Later, 72 Squadron, also located at Odiham, started to equip with the type just two months later. The helicopter provided the RAF's all-important capability for troop and freight transport, paratrooping, supply-dropping, casualty evacuation, and any other kind of requirement associated with its Army cooperation duties. As an ambulance, the Belvedere could accommodate eight to twelve stretcher cases while as a freighter it could carry 6,000 lb. Bulky loads of up to 5,250 lb, which could not be accommodated inside the fuselage, were slung from a strong point underneath it.

On a unique mission in April 1962, a Belvedere HC.1 (XG465) from 72 Squadron was used to lift and position an 80-foot bronze lattice spire onto the roof of the Sir Basil Spence's newly constructed Coventry Cathedral, built upon the ashes of the old cathedral that had burnt to the ground in a devastating raid by German bombers in 1942. Once in position on its mounting plinth, the spire was bolted into position. The delicate operation was performed by Squadron Leader John Dowling, Flight Lieutenant Ron Salt and Flight Lieutenant J. Martin.

Argosy joins 114 Squadron

The first Argosy aircraft reached the Operational Conversion Unit (OCU) at RAF Benson in November 1961. In February of the following year, 114 Squadron (also at Benson) became the first squadron to equip with the new type. From 1963, Argosy C.1 aircraft equipped both the Middle East and Far East Air Forces, and they were capable of air-to-air refuelling from Victor tankers. All fifty-six Argosy aircraft were delivered by April 1964.

The Argosy C.1 combined the roles of a main airlift vehicle with a tactical transport aircraft. A robust undercarriage enabled it to operate from semi-prepared surfaces, while it was capable of short take-off and landing runs. The raised flight deck accommodated a first and second pilot, a navigator and a flight engineer, plus a supernumerary crew seat. A distinctive feature of the Argosy was the 'crocodile-jaw' supply doors in the rear fuselage which could be opened in flight for supply drops. In normal trooping operations, with sixty-nine fully-equipped men aboard, the loading-door area was used to accommodate kit-bags. A wide range of Army vehicles and guided weapons could also be accommodated.

New Comet joins the Command

The first Comet C.4 (XR395) made its first flight at Hawarden on 15 November 1961 and was delivered to RAF Lyneham in February 1962. The remaining four aircraft were delivered by the end of 1962.

The Comet C.4 was a military version of the civilian Comet 4C. It accommodated ninety-four passengers instead of forty-four in the C.2 and could be distinguished by the longer fuselage (118 feet) and wing tanks. It was powered by four 10,500 lb static thrust Avon 350 turbojets. Maximum cruising speed was 503 mph (480 mph in C.2) and gross weight 162,000 lb (120,000 lb in C.2).

Andover C.1 ordered

The Andover C.1 was a military development of the Avro 748 civil transport which first appeared in 1960. It was designed (as the Avro 780) to meet an RAF operational requirement for a multi-purpose transport aircraft with STOL capability, available for troop transport, paratrooping, aerial delivery of supplies, freighting, aero-medical evacuation and long-range ferry. The Andover met this requirement admirably, operating from rough airstrips, ploughed fields or desert strips as short as 300 yards in length. It differed from its civil counterpart in having more powerful Rolls-Royce Dart turboprop engines with larger-diameter airscrews, a lengthened rear fuselage with rear-loading facilities and a 'beaver' tail for air dropping. A unique characteristic was its 'kneeling' undercarriage, which enabled the fuselage angle to be raised or lowered so that vehicles of various sizes (from armoured cars to Land Rovers) could be driven on or off the rear-loading ramp.

In 1962, the sole production order for thirty-one Andover C.1 tactical transport aircraft was contracted to Hawker Siddeley Aviation Ltd at Woodford. The prototype (XS594) was set to fly in July 1965.

The winter of '63

The 'Big Freeze of 1963' was one of the coldest winters on record in the UK. Temperatures plummeted and lakes and rivers began to freeze over. In the Central England Temperature (CET) record, which extends back to 1659, only the winter of 1683/84 has been significantly colder than that of 1963.

Throughout the severe winter, RAF rescue helicopters flew daily missions in many parts of the west and north of the UK providing fodder for cattle and food for villagers, many of whom had been completely cut off by heavy snow. They also flew GPO engineers (General Post Office, who installed and maintained the telephone system across the UK) to discover and repair breaks in telephone lines. They also flew Electricity Board officials for the repair of electricity grid lines.

Around the time, 230 Squadron was just at the point of completing its conversion from Single and Twin Pioneers to Whirlwind helicopters at the end of 1962. Those eleven Whirlwinds held on strength were being prepared for the move to RAF Gutersloh in January 1963. However, a note in their Form 540 from January 1963 reports: 'Instead of moving the Squadron to Germany as expected on the 1st January the cold and snowy weather in the UK produced some interesting tasks for the helicopters. On 1st January four Whirlwind left Odiham for Chivenor in answer to a call from 19 Group to help in rescue and relief work. They were joined later by two more.'

Thankfully, the thaw set in during early March and 6 March enjoyed the first recorded morning of the year without frost anywhere in Britain. The temperatures soon soared to 17 °C and the remaining snow rapidly disappeared – gone but not forgotten!

Operation Triplex

During September–October 1963, Transport Command was once again supporting a large exercise being held in and around Libya, this time named Operation Triplex. The major part was held between 1 and 9 October and was based at El Adam and the Tobruk target complex, although the warm-up phase had started on 27 September. Transport Command had been operating in support of squadrons from both Fighter and Bomber Command along with the Far East Air Force and assets from the Royal Navy.

Queen inspects Transport Command on 21st Anniversary

HM the Queen carried out an inspection of Transport Command aircraft at RAF Thorney Island on 27 July 1964, during the Command's 21st Anniversary year. A large static display of aircraft was arranged along the length of Thorney Island's runway 06/24 and featured aircraft from all of Transport Command's UK-based squadrons. The display was concluded with a stream take-off over Transport Command aircraft and a series of set-piece demonstrations by four Wessex helicopters from 72 Squadron.

A change of Government

In October 1964, a new Labour Government under Harold Wilson assumed office following the result of the General Election held on 15 October. It was a crushing blow to the previous Conservative Government, who had held office since 1951. One of their first actions was to carry out a searching Defence Review which was to have major consequences for all three services. Changes inaugurated in 1965–66 would eventually lead to the end of Transport Command as it had been known since 1943.

An unidentified Transport Command Beverley C.1 aircraft landing at Tmimi in Libya, during Exercise Starlight in March 1960. (*Crown Copyright/ Air Historical Branch T-1768*)

Troops load a Land Rover and trailer onto a Blackburn Beverley C.1 transport at Tmimi in the Libyan desert, to be airlifted to a forward location during Exercise Starlight in March 1960. (*Crown Copyright/Air Historical Branch T-1716*)

Twin Pioneer CC.1s of 230 Squadron (including XL996) photographed while operating in the Libyan desert during Exercise Starlight in March 1960. (*Crown Copyright/ Air Historical Branch T-1721*)

A line of Westland Whirlwind HAR.10 helicopters of 225 Squadron at El Adem, Libya, in March 1960 during Exercise Starlight. To the left is XD165/K in yellow 'Rescue' colours while XK991/J is the first camouflaged example in the line. (*Crown Copyright/ Air Historical Branch T-1748*)

Engineers use a mobile crane to remove the giant rear cargo door of a 47 Squadron Beverley C.1, XB265, at El Adem, Libya, during Exercise Starlight in 1960. (*Crown Copyright/Air Historical Branch T-1709*)

A pair of Transport Command Hasting aircraft pass over the summit of Mount Kilimanjaro, Tanzania, in 1961. The aircraft are WD477, a C.2 of 36 Squadron (nearest), and TG605, a C.1 of 114 Squadron. At the time of the photograph, both squadrons were based at RAF Colerne, but in September 1961, 114 Squadron was disbanded and reformed at RAF Benson as the first squadron to receive the Argosy C.1. (*Crown Copyright/Air Historical Branch CMP-1233*)

An unidentified Beverley C.1 (coded 'B') with two Hastings aircraft of Transport Command at an airfield in Kuwait during Operation Vantage. (*Crown Copyright/Air Historical Branch CMP-1242*)

A Beverley C.1 of 30 Squadron dropping sacks of food to Kenyan people whose territory was devastated by severe floods during November 1961. Four Beverley aircraft from numbers 47 and 53 Squadrons based at RAF Abingdon joined the four-month-long relief effort on 18 November when they airlifted Sycamores of 225 Squadron into Nairobi airport. During their time in Kenya, the Beverley aircraft dropped a total of 715 tons of food. The RAF element of the multinational effort was known as Operation Tana Flood. (*Crown Copyright/Air Historical Branch CMP-1320*)

Bristol Belvedere HC.1 helicopters of the Belvedere Trials Unit, based at RAF Odiham. Three helicopters featured in this photograph are XG456/C, XF453/A and XG454/B. All were part of the batch of nine pre-production Belvederes ordered by the RAF. In September 1961, the Trials Unit was re-formed as 66 Squadron and briefly served as a unit within Transport Command. (*Crown Copyright/Air Historical Branch T-2569*)

An unusual view of two Armstrong Whitworth Argosy C.1 aircraft of 114 Squadron at RAF Benson, photographed on 13 March 1962 from the open rear ramp of another Argosy aircraft. (*Crown Copyright/Air Historical Branch T-2990*)

De Havilland Comet C.2, XK715 *Columba*, of 216 Squadron, photographed at RAF Gan in the Indian Ocean, during 1962. It is thought that the red bands may have been applied to the aircraft while it was loaned to 51 Squadron between May and September 1962. (*Crown Copyright/Air Historical Branch T-3301*)

HRH the Duke of York inspects a line-up of RAF transport aircraft at RAF Odiham on 26 October 1962 including Beverley C.1 XB288 and Britannia C.1 XL658 *Adkara*, along with a Comet C.4, Comet C.2 and Belfast C.1. (*Crown Copyright/Air Historical Branch PRB-1-24127*)

The infamous winter of 1963. Residents of Simonsbath, on the edge of the Exmoor National Park, approach a Whirlwind HAR.10 of 230 Squadron (XP402/X) which has just landed with relief supplies in January of 1963. In what were believed to be the largest operations of their kind to have been undertaken by the RAF, helicopters from numbers 225 and 230 Squadrons at RAF Odiham, along with 22 Squadron at RAF Chivenor, transported people stranded in remote areas while Transport Command Beverley C.1 aircraft dropped cattle fodder to aid farmers. (*Crown Copyright/Air Historical Branch PRB-1-24459*)

In 1962, five Comet C.4 aircraft (XR395–399) were delivered to 216 Squadron at RAF Lyneham to supplement the Comet C.2 aircraft already in service. The Comet C.4 could be distinguished by its longer fuselage and could accommodate ninety-four passengers instead of forty-four in the C.2. Comet C.4 XR397 was photographed in March 1963. (*Crown Copyright/Air Historical Branch T-3695*)

A marshaller guides the pilot of a 225 Squadron Whirlwind HAR.10 helicopter, XP338, into position to lift a small underslung load during night training at RAF Odiham in mid-1963. (*Crown Copyright/Air Historical Branch T-4008*)

225 Squadron Whirlwind HAR.10 helicopters from RAF Odiham, photographed while training on Salisbury Plain in mid-1963. Featured in this picture are XP338/P, XP359/K, XP339/G and XP363/W. (*Crown Copyright/Air Historical Branch T-4013*)

Ground crew servicing a Hawker Hunter FGA.9 aircraft of 1 Squadron at El Adem, Libya, during Exercise Triple West, a major air mobility exercise held in September and October of 1963. (*Crown Copyright/Air Historical Branch CMP-1413*)

An interesting formation flown over RAF Lyneham in May 1964. It was led by Britannia C.1 XM519, followed by 216 Squadron Comet C.4 XR396 and Comet C.2 XK698. Elsewhere on the field are ten further Britannia C.1 aircraft along with a Comet C.2. (*Crown Copyright/ Air Historical Branch PRB-1-28739*)

WV736, one of the Pembroke C.1 VIP aircraft used by the Metropolitan Communications Squadron at RAF Northolt in 1964. In addition to its VIP duties, the squadron's aircraft were frequently used by officers working at the Air Ministry in Central London to maintain their flying currency. (*Crown Copyright/ Air Historical Branch T-4314*)

A spectacular night image of Britannia C.1, XL658, pictured at RAF Lyneham in 1964. The Britannia C.1 fleet was pooled between numbers 99 and 511 Squadrons at the base. (*Crown Copyright/Air Historical Branch X-87032*)

A giant Blackburn Beverley C.1 transport aircraft – XL130 – is moved into a hangar using a special trolley to allow for routine maintenance. The trolley allows the aircraft to be tipped so that the tailplane sits below height of the hangar doors. (*Crown Copyright/ Air Historical Branch T-4436*)

The first Short Belfast C.1, XR362, pictured at the manufacturer's factory at Sydenham, Belfast, in 1964, prior to its delivery to 53 Squadron at RAF Brize Norton. (*Crown Copyright/Air Historical Branch T-4376*)

Andover, Belfast and VC10 (1965–67)

The third Belfast C.1, XR364, photographed during a pre-delivery test flight in March 1965. Some 25 per cent larger than the Lockheed Hercules (which entered RAF service in 1967), the Belfast could carry a greater payload than the American design and was capable of accommodating three Whirlwind or two Wessex helicopters. It was the first military transport with a fully automatic landing system. (*Crown Copyright/Air Historical Branch T-5365*)

Though eagerly awaited as another step in the new Government's rethinking of defence commitments and expenditure, the Statement on Defence Estimates 1965, published on 23 February 1965, contained no startling developments. The big decisions were already known.

It was, of course, the first defence White Paper issued under the unified 'Tri-Service' Ministry of Defence, formed on 1 April 1964, and the first under the new Labour Government. Unlike the infamous White Paper of 1957, which tried to reorganise defence in one blow and proved wrong in almost every major point, this White Paper made the point that reorganisation must be a progressive process.

Total estimates for defence expenditure in the coming year were given as £2,120.5 million, an increase in 'real terms' of 2.3 per cent over those of the previous year. Of the total, the RAF defence allocation was £561.77m and for the Ministry of Aviation it was £254.67m. The total defence bill was equivalent to £39 per head of the British population – almost as much as the per head expenditure on tobacco and alcohol.

Oil airlift into Zambia

Following the Rhodesian Unilateral Declaration of Independence (UDI) on 11 November 1965, ten Javelins of 29 Squadron were detached from their base at RAF Akrotiri, Cyprus, to Ndola in Zambia (formerly Northern Rhodesia) early in 1966 to provide air defence against possible attacks from the former Southern Rhodesia, which had had a series of United Nations sanctions imposed against Ian Smith's government. 51 Squadron, RAF Regiment was also flown in from Catterick, North Yorkshire, to secure airfields and important installations (such as the Kariba Dam power station, which straddles the border between the two countries) along with mobile air control equipment and personnel. The fighters arrived at Eastleigh airport in Nairobi on 1 December, in anticipation of a formal request by the government of Kenneth Kaunda, which eventually arrived the following day.

Alongside the air defence tasks, an airlift was started to fly oil into Zambia as the UN sanctions against Rhodesia had forced the only supply line into the country to be cut off. Between 20 December 1965 and 31 October 1966, RAF Britannia C.1 aircraft of 99 and 511 Squadrons, known locally as 'Mushroom Airways', flew an average of 275 barrels per day into the country from Dar-es-Salaam in Tanzania, with each aircraft capable of carrying a 21,000 lb load in fifty full drums (2,250 gallons) in and ninety-two empty drums out. Somewhat ironically, the airlift was almost self-defeating as each RAF Britannia C.1 consumed around 2,700 gallons of fuel for each return journey of six and a half hours. This was in addition to flying passengers and freight to support the Javelins and ground forces. The unloading and loading of aircraft, which eventually included a small number of civilian aircraft including Channel Bridge Air Ferry ATL-98 Carvairs and CC-130E Hercules aircraft of the Royal Canadian Air Force (RCAF), was carried out by teams from the Mobile Air Movements Squadron detached from Abingdon, Cyprus and Aden to Ndola and Lusaka.

Food dropping Argosy

The winter of 1965/66 once again provided copious quantities of snow around the country. So much so, that Barford Camp, the Army's military accommodation base near Barnard Castle in County Durham, was completely cut off. A supply drop was organised at short notice and was flown by an Argosy C.1 of 267 Squadron from RAF Benson. A report in 267 Squadron's Form 540 at the time records: 'Sortie undertaken on 1 December 1965 after heavy snow had cut off the army camp at Barnard Castle. Argosy XN848 was used to drop supplies to the troops successfully and, in the process, received considerable publicity in the popular press, seventeen of whom flew in an accompanying aircraft (XR135) to take pictures. This gained the unofficial title Operation Snowdrop in the following day's papers.'

Delivery of the Belfast to 53 Squadron

With delivery of its first Belfast C.1 (XR367) to 53 Squadron at RAF Brize Norton on 20 January 1966, the RAF became the first air force in the world to operate a military transport aircraft with a fully automatic landing system. The Belfast was also the first British aircraft ever designed from the outset for the long-range military transport role.

The prototype Belfast, originally with civil registration G-ASKE but later allocated the serial XR362, made its first flight at the company's airfield at Sydenham on 5 January 1964. Ten were ordered for the RAF with serials in the range XR362 to 371 inclusive, with the final aircraft (XR371) being delivered to 53 Squadron at the end of 1966.

Andover C.1 enters service

After the prototype Andover C.1 (XS594) had made its first flight on 9 July 1965, the type began to enter service with the RAF in December 1966. At home it was issued to 46 Squadron at RAF Abingdon and overseas it went to 52 Squadron of the Far East Air Force, based at Seletar, Singapore. A total of thirty-one Andover aircraft were built for the RAF with serials in the ranges XS594–613 and XS637–647.

Delivery of first VC-10 C.1 to 10 Squadron

The military version of the VC-10 was produced to RAF Specification C239 of 1960. An initial order for five was announced in September 1961, followed by a further six in 1962 and a final three in July 1964. In overall dimensions it was the same as the civil-standard VC-10, but incorporated the up-rated Rolls-Royce Conway engines and the additional fuel capacity (located in the tail fin) of the Super VC-10. Modifications unique to the RAF variant included a side-loading freight door, strengthened floor, rearward-facing seats, an in-flight refuelling probe and a Bristol Siddeley Artouste auxiliary power unit (APU) mounted in the tail cone.

The first VC-10 C.1 for the RAF (XR806) made its initial flight at Weybridge on 26 November 1965. First deliveries to the RAF took place in July 1966. 10 Squadron, initially based at RAF Fairford and later at RAF Brize Norton, operated the VC-10 C.1 fleet. The first overseas training flight (by XR808) flew to Hong Kong in August 1966, and the first regular route flights started on 4 April 1967. Eventually, VC-10 C.1 aircraft operated twenty-seven flights per month to the Far East via the Persian Gulf. The VC-10 C.1s of 10 Squadron, nicknamed 'Shiny Tens' because of the finish on the aircraft, shared their Brize Norton base with the Belfast C.1s of 53 Squadron.

With the arrival of the VC-10 C.1, fourteen of which had entered service with the RAF by the end of 1967, a significant new addition was made to the strategic long-range force of Transport Command and its airlift capacity.

First Hercules C.1 aircraft entering service at RAF Thorney Island

The first of sixty-six Hercules C.1 transport aircraft had arrived with Marshalls of Cambridge in December 1966. The first aircraft entered service with 242 Operational Conversion Unit (OCU) in April 1967 at RAF Thorney Island.

Shortly afterwards, the first operational unit (36 Squadron) received its aircraft on 1 August 1967 at RAF Lyneham. Further deliveries were made to RAF Lyneham in 1968 including 24 Squadron in February, 47 Squadron in March and 30 Squadron in June.

Airlift out of Aden

On 3 May 1967, an urgent evacuation of service families from Aden began and was completed by 20 July. Within six months of the start of the airlift all British troops and aircraft had left the Federation for ever. The entire evacuation was a triumph of careful planning and an event of historical importance as the biggest RAF airlift since Berlin. There were complicating factors: a distinct possibility that the final stages might turn into a 'fighting withdrawal'; the looming crisis between Turkey and Greece over Cyprus – a vital staging post on the strategic air route; and finally the need to retain flexibility in the timing of each and every phase of the operation.

The tactical airlift from Aden in the final three days of withdrawal was provided by Hercules and Britannia aircraft flying a 1,000-mile leg to RAF Muharraq on Bahrain Island. Here, troops handed in their weapons, ate and bathed before re-embarking for the strategic airlift back to the UK by RAF VC-10 C.1 and Britannia aircraft, supplemented by three civilian VC-10 flights operated by British United Airways (BUA) under military charter.

One of the secrets of the success of the whole operation was the positioning, at Aden and Bahrain, of the two Air Support Command operation cells to work in conjunction with the forward Air Transport Operations Centre. Two Belfast C.1 aircraft were also employed in the operation as well as 105 Squadron Argosy C.1 aircraft which carried out six shuttle flights each day between Khormaksar and all Gulf airfields.

The role of Muharraq as the hub for the withdrawal was crucial. Tactical transport aircraft (Hercules, Argosy and Britannia) moved men and machines into Muharraq from where strategic transport aircraft (VC-10, Britannia and Belfast) flew them back into the UK.

Renamed Air Support Command

The change from Transport Command to Air Support Command on 11 August 1967 was not just a change of name but of operational concept. The searching review of Defence policy undertaken by the new Labour Government when they came to power in October 1964 had considered the former Imperial commitments and, in the words of the Defence Estimates 1967, had aimed 'to foster developments which will enable local peoples to live at peace without the presence of external forces' – thereby permitting British Forces to withdraw from the Middle and the Far East, as well as Aden.

However, this policy was not without its implications. Britain should maintain obligations to friends and allies across the world and should retain a capacity for contributing to the maintenance of peace – a Rapid Reaction Force. The Supplementary Statement on Defence Policy 1967 stated: 'In the next decade, new aircraft will enable us to move forces across the world faster and in larger numbers than was possible even a few years ago.'

However, the role and title of 'Transport Command' did not accurately represent this new role and the title of 'Air Support Command' was considered more appropriate to moving the new 'Air Mobility Force' wherever it may be required.

The change of name appears to have had little or no effect at squadron level as roles and tasks remained much the same; it was only the Command name on the side of the aircraft that had changed.

On 11 August 1967, Air Support Command inherited the following squadrons and equipment from Transport Command:

10 Andover C.1	(eight in 46 Squadron and two on loan to the OCU)
10 Belfast C.1	(53 Squadron)
20 Argosy C.1	(numbers 114 and 267 Squadrons)
10 Beverley C.1	(47 Squadron)
5 Comet C.4	(216 Squadron)
14 Hastings C.1	(24 Squadron)
9 Hercules C.1	(in use with OCU before being delivered to 36 Squadron)
14 VC10 C.1	(10 Squadron)
23 Britannia C.1	(numbers 99 and 511 Squadrons)
24 Hunter GA.9	(numbers 1 and 54 Squadrons)
20 Wessex HC.2	(72 Squadron)
10 Whirlwind HAR.10	(230 Squadron)

It was a formidable force and demonstrated that in the final years of its distinguished existence, Transport Command had become a powerful and effective arm for the nation's mobile, ever-ready defence forces.

The Headquarters RAF Transport Command control room, photographed on 17 August 1965. (*Crown Copyright/Air Historical Branch PRB-1-31344*)

XR806 was the very first VC10 C.1 for the RAF. It was photographed with its Transport Command titles outside of the main production area at Brooklands in February 1965, ahead of its first flight, which was made on the 26th. (*BAE SYSTEMS Image Ref MP24169*)

A Blackburn Beverley C.1 of Transport Command on a temporary airstrip during Exercise Slip Pillow, a combined operation exercise held at Barrybudden on the Firth of Tay during April 1965. (*Crown Copyright/Air Historical Branch T-8258*)

To mark the occasion of the award of their first Standard on 25 June 1965, 114 Squadron, RAF Benson, flew a three-ship Argosy C.1 formation featuring XR142, XN856 and XN847. (*Crown Copyright/Air Historical Branch T-5566*)

De Havilland Comet C.4, XR399, of 216 Squadron, on a snow-covered flightline at Narvik, Norway, in 1965. (*Crown Copyright/Air Historical Branch T-5637*)

Argosy C.1, XN848, of 267 Squadron, RAF Benson, photographed while air-dropping supplies to Barford Camp, the Army's military accommodation base near Barnard Castle in County Durham on 1 December 1965, after it had been cut off by heavy snow. (*Crown Copyright/ Air Historical Branch T-5988*)

Belfast C.1, XR367, of 53 Squadron, RAF Brize Norton, photographed on the flightline at Muharraq, Bahrain, in 1966. (*Crown Copyright/Air Historical Branch CMP-1525*)

A corporal of the Mobile Air Movements Squadron positions a freight lift platform with the aid of local labourers to allow the unloading of a Britannia C.1 (XM490 *Aldebaran*) at Embakazi during the oil airlift into Zambia. (*Crown Copyright/Air Historical Branch PRB-1-32482*)

A view inside a Britannia C.1 loaded with fifty full 45-gallon oil barrels on its arrival at Embakazi. To preserve the floor, copious amounts of wood chippings were spread and numerous restraining chains used to keep the barrels – carefully loaded in six piles of eight plus, if no passengers were flying, a further pair towards the rear of the cabin – in place. (*Crown Copyright/Air Historical Branch PRB-1-32484*)

For many years the Pembroke C.1s of Transport Command were familiar sights at RAF airfields in the UK and Germany, operating on VIP and liaison duties. This aircraft – WV746 – was on the strength of the Western Communications Squadron at RAF Andover at the time of this image in December 1966. The squadron, which formed on 1 April 1964, came about after the merger of the Maintenance Command Communication and Ferry Squadron with the Training Command Communication Squadron. (*Crown Copyright/Air Historical Branch T-6858*)

Shortly after delivery to 10 Squadron, then based at RAF Fairford, VC10 C.1 XR808 commenced crew standardisation trials before operating route proving flights to Hong Kong, where it was photographed on 23 August 1966. (*Crown Copyright/Air Historical Branch T-6677*)

The Andover C.1 was a military development of the Avro 748 civil transport which first appeared in 1960, and later a total of thirty-one were ordered by the RAF. It entered RAF service in June 1966 with 242 Operational Conversion Unit at RAF Thorney Island, before squadron deliveries commenced to Transport Command in September. Initially, it was delivered to 46 Squadron whose colours adorn the three aircraft pictured (XS603, XS604 and XS605) at around the time of the unit's arrival at RAF Abingdon in September 1966. (*Crown Copyright/Air Historical Branch T-6871*)

The Lockheed Hercules C.1 was ordered by the RAF to replace the Hastings and Beverley as the standard medium-range tactical transport aircraft. The first of sixty-six Hercules for the RAF (XV176) made its first flight at the Lockheed production facility at Marietta, Georgia, on 19 October 1966. The first Hercules C.1 to be delivered was XV177, which arrived at Marshalls of Cambridge on 19 December 1966, where this photograph was taken. The aircraft, delivered in natural metal finish, was then fitted out with its communication equipment and painted into the Transport Command camouflage of the time: 'dark earth' and 'mid stone' with black undersides. (*Crown Copyright/Air Historical Branch T-6885*)

A pair of Basset CC.1 aircraft, XS777 and XS778, of the Southern Communications Squadron, RAF Bovingdon, in 1967. Despite the close proximity to the handover to RAF Support Command, both aircraft still carried the RAF Transport Command titles on the nose. (*Crown Copyright/Air Historical Branch T-7410*)

By the second half of the 1960s, Transport Command's fleet of long-range aircraft saw the introduction of several new types of greater capability. Four of the Command's strategic transport force of 'shiny' aircraft were gathered at RAF Fairford for this photograph taken in April 1967. Clockwise from left to right are: VC-10 C.1 XR807 (*Donald Garland VC/Thomas Grey VC*) of 10 Squadron; Comet C.4 XR396 of 216 Squadron; Britannia C.1 XM520 (*Arcturus*) of 99/511 Squadron; and Belfast C.1 XR365 (*Ajax*) of 53 Squadron. (*Crown Copyright/Air Historical Branch T-7157*)

The first of the new Lockheed Hercules C.1 aircraft to actually enter service with RAF Transport Command was XV179, which was photographed in the 'dark earth and mid-stone' camouflage on 5 June 1967. (*Crown Copyright/Air Historical Branch T-7190*)

Transport Command becomes Air Support Command. Air Support Command's last two Beverley aircraft made a farewell flypast over the Command Headquarters at RAF Upavon on 6 December 1967, before flying on to 21 Maintenance Unit at RAF Shawbury to be placed in storage. Both aircraft – XB269/F and XB290/X – still wore the markings of 47 Squadron. (*Crown Copyright/Air Historical Branch T-7857*)

Bibliography

British Aviation Research Group, *British Military Aircraft Serials and Markings*, 2nd Edition, BARG/Nostalgair/The Aviation Hobby Shop, 1983.

Ellis, Ken, *Wrecks & Relics*, 24th Edition, Crécy Publishing, 2014.

Flintham, Victor, *Air Wars and Aircraft – A detailed Record of Air Combat, 1945 to the present*, Arms and Armour Press, 1989.

Flintham, Vic and Thomas, Andrew, *Combat Codes – A Full Explanation And Listing Of British, Commonwealth and Allied Air Force Unit Codes Since 1938*, Pen & Sword Aviation, 2008.

Hamlin, John F., *The de Havilland Dragon/Dragon Rapide Family*, Air Britain (Historians) Limited, 2003.

Jefford MBE RAF, Wing Commander C.G., *RAF Squadrons*, Airlife, 1988.

Lee, Air Chief Marshal Sir David, *Flight from the Middle East*, Ministry of Defence, 1978.

Richie, Dr Sebastian, *The RAF, Small Wars and Insurgencies: Later Colonial Operations, 1945–1975*, Air Historical Branch, 2011.

Robertson, Bruce, *British Military Aircraft Serials 1878–1987*, Midland Counties Publications, 1987.

Thetford, Owen, *Aircraft of the Royal Air Force since 1918*, 8th Edition, Putnam, 1988.

Wilson, Keith, *RAF in Camera: 1950s*, Pen & Sword Aviation, 2015.

Wilson, Keith, *RAF in Camera: 1960s*, Pen & Sword Aviation, 2015.

Wilson, Keith, *Vickers/BAC VC10 Manual*, Haynes Publishing, 2016.

Wynn, Humphrey, *Forged in War – A History of RAF Transport Command 1943–1967*, The Stationery Office, 1996.

Magazines:

Various editions of *Air Clues* magazine, issued monthly for the Royal Air Force by the Director of Flying Training (MoD).

The National Archives:

Various historical records, official reports and Form 540s from a variety of RAF squadrons and stations.